William Farquhar

Poems on Several Occasions

William Farquhar
Poems on Several Occasions
ISBN/EAN: 9783337006013

Printed in Europe, USA, Canada, Australia, Japan

Cover: Foto ©Thomas Meinert / pixelio.de

More available books at **www.hansebooks.com**

POEMS

ON

SEVERAL OCCASIONS.

POEMS

ON

SEVERAL OCCASIONS:

CONSISTING OF

ELEGIES
&
EPISTLES,

MISCELLANIES
&
SCOTTISH PIECES.

By WM. FARQUHAR.

Curs'd be the Verse, how well foe'er it flow,
Which tends to make one worthy man my foe,
Gives Virtue scandal, Innocence a fear,
Or from the soft-ey'd Virgin steals a tear.
                                        POPE.

EDINBURGH:
PRINTED FOR THE AUTHOR,

1794.

ADVERTISEMENT.

THE Author of the following Poems had resolved to allow his performance to appear without any Dedication; but being, on his arrival at Edinburgh, strongly impressed with the public spirited exertions of the Noble Band of Gentlemen, who have armed and embodied themselves, in support of the Government and the Laws of their Country; he has presumed, on the present occasion, to express his high sense of their Worth, by inscribing his performance to them, fully assured, that he could no where meet with more Honourable Patronage.

TO THE RIGHT HONOURABLE
SIR JAMES STIRLING, BARONET,
LORD PROVOST AND LORD LIEUTENANT

OF

THE CITY OF EDINBURGH,

AND

COLONEL

OF

THE EDINBURGH VOLUNTEERS:

AND TO

THE OFFICERS AND GENTLEMEN

WHO COMPOSE

THAT HONOURABLE AND PATRIOTIC BAND.

My Lord and Gentlemen,

Impressed with a deep senfe of your exalted and worthy behaviour, permit an humble Author to lay his little Performance at your feet, with the fond hope that you would accept of it, as an expreffion of his moft profound and fincere admiration, of that Noble Ardour which has called forth your exertions, in behalf of the neareft and deareft Privileges of Society.

To do juftice to your merit, is furely an arduous undertaking; but it affords, at the fame time, a pleafing reflection to the Author of this piece, to behold fo many of the moft worthy of the Citizens of Edinburgh, refolutely ftanding up in defence of true and genuine Liberty, in opposition to that mad and tyrannic Political Frenzy, which has dared to arrogate the sacred title of Freedom, and which misleads its followers and supporters into the mazes of Anarchy and Ruin.

That Britain may still be preserved from the direful effects of such Political Frenzy; and that the subjects of our Gracious Sovereign, may imitate the shining example of Patriotism and Public Spirit, which you, Gentlemen, have exhibited to their view, is the Author's most sincere and ardent wish.

Sensible of the many and great advantages which must accrue to him and his performance, by the honour of having your names prefixed to it,—permit him, Gentlemen, to express his most sincere wishes, that Heaven may invariably smile upon you, and promote your happiness in every respect; and that it may bless and prosper your efforts, in support of Public and Private Peace and Happiness, as well as the Prosperity of Society at large, and of every Individual in particular.

I AM,

WITH THE MOST UNFEIGNED RESPECT,

MY LORD AND GENTLEMEN,

Your most Devoted,
And most Obedient Servant,

EDINBURGH,
Nov. 3. 1794.

W. FARQUHAR.

AN ADDRESS

TO THE RIGHT HONOURABLE
SIR JAMES STIRLING, BARONET,
LORD PROVOST AND LORD LIEUTENANT
OF
THE CITY OF EDINBURGH,
AND
COLONEL
OF
THE EDINBURGH VOLUNTEERS:
AND TO
THE OFFICERS AND GENTLEMEN
WHO COMPOSE
THAT HONOURABLE AND PATRIOTIC BAND.

A youthful Bard at your tribunal lays
His humble ſtrains, and thus ſubmiſſive prays;
That you with influence kind would overſhade,
And ſave from critic rage, his harmleſs head;
For unprotected, at your feet he bows,
Nor Patron, Friend, nor Interceſſor knows.
   When griefs on griefs tumultuous would ariſe,
And ſtream in briny torrents from his eyes,
The gentle Muſe he courted, to aſſwage
Their dreadful conflict, and to calm their rage;

Then would his cheeks a languid smile display,
While 'cross his face joy shot a glimmering ray,
Ah! soon extinguish'd in superior gloom,
When back his mind recoil'd, and met its doom.
His features now a brighter smile illumes,
While on your favour fondly he presumes,
To raise from dark obscurity his name,
And point his way, to honour, wealth, and fame.

 See, fair EDINA's Patriotic Bands
Benevolently stretch their friendly hands,
Gently to chear an unknown friendless Bard,
His lays protect, and his fond toils reward;
To brighter prospects kindly bid him soar,
While, by their smiles, misfortune is no more.
Pleas'd with his honest, tho' unpolish'd Muse,
With generous friendship they promote his views.
Rise then, my Muse, thy humble tribute pay,
Alas! 'tis all thou can'st, a grateful lay!

 When horrid Faction Freedom's guise assum'd,
And, boldly daring, with rude force presum'd
To shake the pillars which support the State;
To spread vile Discord, and promote dire Hate
When men, forgetting Reason's rightful sway,
Tumultuous Passion only would obey;
When the wild notions of a *Madman's* brain,
Led simple fools all order to disdain;
To spurn at Justice, and contemn the Law;
To loose each band which held fierce vice in awe;

To scorn Religion, Virtue to despise,
And wildly court Equality and Vice.
Then, nobly bold, to save a sinking land,
All voluntary came Edina's Band;
Their breasts opposing to the furious tide,
Faction and Discord fled on every side;
The field they leave, their Leaders they forsake,
And in their Country's mercy refuge take.
The storm dispell'd, Britannia's Genius smiles,
Gladly reviewing all her Patriot files;
Each breast She swells, with ardour to maintain
Their Country's glory, and bright Freedom's reign.
 While gloomy war his horrid front extends
O'er Britain's Isle, and gentle Commerce bends
Beneath his iron hand; should Trade decay,
And all her treasures seem to waste away,
Yet happier times shall come, when balmy peace
Shall hush dire war, and bid wild Discord cease;
Then to the winds shall Commerce spread her sail,
And Trade and Industry again prevail;
Britannia's glory shall afresh revive,
And every shock of adverse fate survive;
To latest ages shall her glorious name,
Be loud resounded by immortal fame;
Then Art, awakening, shall her toils renew,
And bid new wonders rise to human view;

Then shall the Muse some Poet's breast inspire,
In Britain's praise to tune the sounding lyre;
To sing her triumphs, her bright acts display,
Where'er the sun dispenses chearing day.
Aided by Phœbus and the gentle Muse,
Your Patriot deeds the Poet shall diffuse,
And justly tell to latest times your fame,
And load with honours due your worthy Name,
Who thus have boldly dar'd rude war's alarms,
And in your Country's cause are found in arms.

THE PREFACE.

It would be both unneceſſary and mean, in the Author of the following POEMS, to endeavour to conceal from the Public the motives which have induced him to appear in print: And he defpifes the conduct of thofe, who endeavour to befpeak the favour of the Public, by the hackneyed method of alleging, that they have publiſhed their Performances at the earneſt and repeated requeſt of Friends.

Neither vanity, nor the defire of praife, have influenced him on the prefent occafion; but a laudable wiſh of endeavouring to do juſtice to fome claims on him, which he had no other means of fatisfying.

Having thus difclofed his motives in the prefent Publication, he hopes that the Public will, with its accuſtomed generofity, enable him to carry his views into execution.

He aſſures thofe who have fubfcribed for this Performance, that it can at leaſt challenge the merit of being friendly, on every occasion, to the interests of Virtue.

What other excellence it possesses, must be determined by the voice of the Public, to whose decision its Author has submitted it.

If there are, either in the language, or the sentiments of these POEMS, any great faults, the candid part of my Readers, will impute these to the inexperience of their Author, and will be more ready to palliate or excuse them, when they are informed, that he has not as yet completed his twenty-third year; and that by far the greater number of these Pieces were composed between the sixteenth and eighteenth years of his age. Indeed, they were written to soothe the langour of a vacant hour, or for the amusement of some particular acquaintance, without either a wish or intention that they should appear in Print.

As there is, in one Piece, a part which the Author cannot call his own, though he is under no apprehension of being called a Plagiarist upon its account; yet he thinks it necessary to own, that it was not entirely composed by him, lest the Writer of the two first parts should have communicated it to any of his Friends; for he is perfectly sensible, that he now has neither the inclination nor the ability to have completed it, as he voluntarily resigned that task to the Author, and allowed him to print it wholly as his own.

It may not, perhaps, be a favourable circumstance for this Performance, that it will appear without any Protector: But as the worthy Person, whom the Author had singled out as its Patron, has declined to accept the task, he has resolved to leave it entirely to the generosity of the Public, without attempting to shelter it from the shaft of criticism, under the name of any person whatsoever.

From the benevolent and feeling part of Mankind, it has nothing to fear; and it is not meant for persons of a different description.

If it shall not meet with the approbation of the Public, its Author's only regret will be, that he should receive money for that which the Purchaser did not, upon perusal, deem a competent recompence, either for his trouble in reading, or his expence in buying. As an Author, he will be but little affected, as this is his first, and, he sincerely hopes, shall be his last appearance in that character.

THE

CONTENTS.

ELEGIES.

	Page
I. To the memory of Miss S. Gordon	9
II. To the memory of George Rait	10
III. To the memory of James Rait	11
IV. Another to the memory of G. Rait	13
V. To the memory of Miss P. Eagliftone	15
VI. To the memory of the private Pantheon Society,	16
VII. To the memory of my Hat, loft in a voyage at fea	18
VIII. The complaint of delicacy	20
IX. On difcontent	23
X. To fenfibility	25
XI. On human life	27
XII. Addreffed to fortune	29

EPISTLES.

I. To Mr Andrew Sheriffs, printer	33
II. To Mr Geo. Cruden	40
III. To Mr John Moir, printer	46
IV. To Mr John Bell, bookfeller, London	52
V. To a Literary Society in Aberdeen	56

EPISTLES.   Page

VI. To Dr Beattie, Professor of Moral Philosophy   63
VII. To Miss N—— P—— at C——n——h   65
VIII. To J—— I—— Aberdeen   -   68
IX. To Mr Andrew Imrey, at Edinburgh   -   71
X. To Mr James Rait, Aberdeen   -   81

MISCELLANIES.

On knowledge   -   -   -   89
Death, a poem   -   -   -   102
The beauties of deformity, a poem   -   106
A paraphrase on the Book of Job. Part I.   -   111
———————————————————Part II.   -   117
———————————————————Part III.   -   123
A tale   -   -   -   -   126
The conquest of vanity   -   -   133
On intemperance   -   -   -   137
Luxury and avarice, a fable, versified from the Spectator   -   -   -   141
On three remarkable occurrences   -   144
Verses, written on seeing the execution of Robert Watt   -   -   -   146
The modern hero   -   -   -   149
The birth of beauty, a fable, versified from the Tatler   -   -   -   153
Extempore, on " *Avarus semper egit*"   -   155
Lines addressed to Miss N—— I—— Aberdeen   157
Parnassus at home   -   -   -   159
The wish   -   -   -   160
Lines addressed to a Young Lady, written at the desire of a friend   -   -   161
Ode to hope   -   -   -   164

SCOTTISH EPISTLES.

	Page
I. To Mr John Moir, printer, Edin.	169
II. To Mr Alex. Scott, Ballhill	171
III. To the Reviewers	174
IV. To Mr Alex. Scott, Ballhill	176

SCOTTISH MISCELLANIES.

Epilogue, spoken at the representation of the Tragedy of Douglas, at Slains	181
Elegy to the memory of a favourite Bitch	183
An Address, intended for the opening of the Author's Circulating Library, Peterhead	186
Horace, Book I. Ode XXVI. imitated	188
A Song	189
A Song	191

ELEGIES.

ELEGY I.

TO THE MEMORY OF
MISS SUSAN GORDON
OF ABERDOUR.

What mournful sounds are these which strike
    mine ear,
And call from Pity's eye the falling tear?
Thy fate a warning to each mind imparts,
Subdu'd by grief behold the hardest hearts.
Where's now, alas! the beautiful, the gay,
Whose eyes once rival'd the bright source of day;
On whose warm cheek the blush of beauty glow'd
And Nature on her form each charm bestow'd?
  So falls a Lilly by the cruel spade,
And in the dust its beauteous colours fade:
Like a tall pine, stretch'd on the verdant mead,
With all its branching honours on its head.
Accept, fair Shade, of this my pensive lay,
The tribute of humanity I pay.

ELEGY II.

TO THE MEMORY OF GEORGE RAIT.

'Twas in the solemn consecrated shade,
Where, in their narrow mansions, rest the dead,
A youth I met, who, with a tearful eye,
Said, " here the ashes of Philander lye !
" Our lov'd, our valu'd Friend is now no more,
" His eyes are clos'd, and the dire struggle's o'er;
" He's past the cares, the little joys of life,
." And 'scap'd this scene of tumult and of strife."
Here ceas'd the youth, and where our Friend was laid,
We mutual pour'd a tribute to his shade.
 O sacred Friendship ! take the pious tear,
Which the muse sheds upon thy mournful bier;
Small is the tribute, tho' the debt not small,
For, while thou liv'dst on earth, thou wast my all ;
In thy society time fled away,
And much too short was summer's longest day.
Still my fond soul had something to impart,
And still thy converse chear'd my pensive heart.

In disappointment's gloom thy counsel stay'd
My heedless steps, and soothing hopes convey'd.
Even when Death frown'd, and beamless was
    thine eye,
Thy conduct taught thy friend how he should die;
With firmest fortitude thou met'st thy fate,
Thy breath resign'd, and gain'd a happier state.

ELEGY III.

TO THE MEMORY OF JAMES RAIT.

AH! dear PHILANDER, when in pensive lay
I mourn'd thy exit from the realms of day,
Ah! little thought I, that a kindred shade
So soon should bid me beg the Muses aid.
Alas! no more her gentle aid avails—
How should she succour when even Physic fails:
Tho' great her power, she cannot Death disarm,
Nor stop the havoc of his ruthless arm;
Beyond his vale, tho' she extends our view.
The dreadful tyrant she could ne'er subdue—
A tyrant did I call him? Ah, my Friend!
Soon may thy arm o'er me the dart extend;

Nor leave me longer in this vale of woe
To mourn the long delay'd, long wiſh'd for blow!
Before each friend I have from earth retire,
By thy kind ſtroke, ah! let me too expire!

When for PHILANDER's fate my tears ſubſide,
His BROTHER's death afreſh renews their tide;
Torn from his friends, decay'd in life's full bloom
He found, alas, too early! found a tomb.
But why thus mourn? miſtaken man, forbear,
Nor let one murmur riſe, nor drop one tear;
Thy friends are ſafe beyond the ſtorms of life,
They've left this ſcene of vanity and ſtrife;
They nature's round in bliſs complete ſurvey;
They've gain'd the realms of everlaſting day.
Safe from our hopes, our fears, our dire alarms,
They're crown'd with bliſs, and never fading charms;
Their kind Creator ſmiles, and bids them ſmile,
Dries all their tears, and buries all their toil.

ELEGY IV.

TO THE MEMORY OF
GEORGE RAIT,

INSERTED IN VOL. 1. OF THE SPECULIST.*

Ah, Dear Philander! thee I mourn,
   For thee I pour my lay;
This plaintive tribute o'er thy urn
   I to thy ashes pay.

Forgotten in the darksome tomb,
   No kind memorial lives
To tell that e'er thou pass'd the womb
   As Nature being gives.

Ah, cruel Death! you pierc'd his heart,
   His heart with virtue stor'd,
Thy steely, thy relentless dart
   Depriv'd us of the hoard.

At thy dire call, from their dark cave
   Diseases throng'd around;
To one you this commission gave,
   One only worthy found.

* Being the Essays of a private society of which he and the author were members.

Thou call'dst, and Pale Confumption came—
  " Go rend PHILANDER's heart:
" Go, flowly fap his youthful frame
  " By thy envenom'd dart."

Thy fervant heard, his wings he fpread,
  And hover'd o'er his prey;
His venom, on PHILANDER fhed,
  Diffolves his mortal clay.

Ah! what avails my plaintive fong,
  PHILANDER is no more!
No more he'll grace our friendly throng,
  Whofe meetings now are o'er.

No more his pen, with folid fenfe
  Shall charm the reader's ear;
Silent his lips, his eloquence
  No more we'll joyful hear.

Nor Virtue's power, nor early worth,
  Could the dire blow award;
Death ftrikes alike at thoughtlefs mirth,
  And thofe whom Virtue guards.

ELEGY V.

TO THE MEMORY OF MISS PEGGY EAGLISTONE.

And can my soul so soon forget
   Her charms, who once awak'd love's fire?
And shall she meet an early fate,
   Yet silent and unsung expire?

No: all your flowers, ye muses, bring,
   To form a garland for her urn;
And let the incense of the spring
   To her untimely grave be born.

Ye Virgins, who her beauty share,
   O'er her the choicest flow'rets strew;
Love shall reward your pious care,
   And give your darling youths to you.

Ye Youths, who pant with fond desire
   Some beauteous virgin's love to gain,
Each one who feels Love's softening fire,
   Or hopes his wishes to obtain.

O'er Peggy's grave freſh roſes ſtrew,
   And teach the myrtle's leaves to ſhade,
Join'd with the willow and the yew,
   The ſacred ſpot where ſhe is laid.

ELEGY VI.

TO THE MEMORY OF
THE PRIVATE PANTHEON SOCIETY.

Can I forget the ſocial friendly few,
   With whom enraptur'd Wiſdom's paths I trode?
Can I forget how ſhe, unveil'd to view,
   Our labours aided, bliſs'd our calm abode?

While Reaſon, ſubject to her mild controul,
   With double energy her power diſplay'd,
And pour'd inſtructive pleaſure on each ſoul,
Or, when vice ſtorm'd, brought virtue ready aid.

Vile Dissipation's giddy joys we scorn'd,
   While Knowledge charm'd, and Virtue bless'd
      our mind;
Pleasing and useful truths our page adorn'd,
   Nor Learning's classic aid was left behind.

When Recollection the sweet scene renews,
   A pleasing pang my pensive bosom feels,
My soul with transport each dear toil reviews,
   While o'er my fancy each past pleasure steals.

But, ah! how scatter'd now, how wide dispers'd,
   Capricious Fortune's fickle smiles to court;
The darling scene is now, alas! revers'd,—
   No more our Members to their Hall resort:

But toss'd on life's wild ocean, find no shore;
   Or, press'd beneath a load of galling woe,
Some seek for bliss in heaps of useless ore,
   Their Patron fallen by Death's relentless blow.

Tho' Fortune to my lot her smile refuse,
   Tho' oft' my brow is wrinkled into frowns,
My pensive mind feels pleasure in the Muse,
   Her sacred influence my soul still owns.

B

From her I learn Fortune to defpife;
  She bids me feek fome calm, fome fweet retreat,
On Virtue's path fhe bids me turn mine eyes,
  Nor wifh the fplendid mis'ry of the great.

What, tho'. I bafk in Fortune's gilded beam,
  If facred Virtue's dictates I difown,
Of real happinefs I only dream,
  If fhe furveys my conduct with a frown.

ELEGY VII.

TO THE MEMORY OF
MY HAT,

LOST IN A VOYAGE BETWEEN LEITH AND MONTROSE, OCT. 1791.

Ah, ever lov'd! ah ever honour'd friend!
  Does fate deny us then one common grave?
Does it command thy ufeful life to end,
  And art thou perifh'd 'mid the azure wave?

Oft' did thy care my *cranium* defend
  From chilling Boreas' rude inclement blaft;
Thy toils, alas! deferv'd a better end,
  Than 'mid the wintry billows to be caft.

Such, such, alas! are the fond hopes of Man—
   Now, high exalted on life's giddy wheel,
He fondly spins eternal plan on plan,
   Nor thinks calamity he e'er shall feel.

Till sudden fate the airy fabric rends,
   Which his fond soul had lull'd to rest secure;
Beneath misfortune's cruel stroke he bends,
   Before he learns its pressure to endure.

Such was thy doom, tho' sleek'd and brush'd with
      skill,
   Too high, alas! thy thoughtless head appear'd
Fearless, unthinking of impending ill,
   Tho' death's dire hand was then against thee
      rear'd.

A cruel rope, the instrument of fate,
   By Boreas press'd against thy lofty crown,
Far from my aid thou lift'st thy head too late,
   While the rude waves assault thy silken down.

Ah, luckless Hat! too good, alas! to shade
   The muse-mad temples of a ragged Bard;
Who now in vain implores thy friendly aid,
   Lest all his wit by chilling blasts be marr'd.

ELEGY VIII.

THE COMPLAINT OF DELICACY.

Begin, my Muse, and touch the tuneful string,
   Till groves and echoing vales resound thy strains,
With head reclin'd, in mourful posture sing,
   How Delicacy left fair Scotia's plains.

What modest Dame, in yonder grove reclin'd,
   With pensive air, and humid eye appears?
What sad ideas, rising in her mind,
   Draw from her lovely eyes the briny tears?

'Tis Delicacy, who here fix'd her seat,
   When by licentious vice chas'd far away,
She form'd this charming, this secure retreat,
   To screen her inj'ries from the light of day.

Here she, with solemn contemplation strays,
   And mourns the scenes which she was forc'd to leave,
And oft' she list's sweet Philomelia's lays,
   Who like herself seem'd only form'd to grieve.

Oft' would she cry, " Ye foolish sons of men,
  " Yet would I gladly press you to my heart,
" Would you be wise, and prove my friends again,
  " I'd honest raptures to your breasts impart.

" Vain, very vain, are all the joys which Vice
  " Upon her silly votaries bestows,
" Would they but trust my candid calm advice,
  " They ne'er would join with their invet'rate
      foes.

" Now Fashion lords it o'er the human mind,
  " Now Pomp and Luxury usurp domain,
" While, leagu'd with Tyranny, with Hate combin'd,
  " They o'er the mind of man unrivall'd reign.

" These my fell foes have chas'd me far from man,
  " And forc'd me in this solitude to dwell,
" While they o'erturn my beneficial plan,
  " I sorrowful must sit in this lone cell.

" Here I unnumber'd miseries must prove,
  " The sure attendants on my helpless fate,
" While, like myself, is banish'd gentle Love,
  " The second victim of man's furious hate.

" My train of timid virtues all retire,
" While in their stead Lust, Passion, Vice, appear,
" And taint man's bosom with corrupt desire,
" Whilst grizly Death and dire Disease draw near."

" These with incessant pangs shall rend man's breast,
" And teach him how to prize departed joy,
" When he, by various crowding ills oppress'd,
" On sensual Pleasure shall begin to cloy.

" Then Health, the offspring of the gods above,
" Shall from his habitation swift retreat,
" Then from his house shall flee all joy and love,
" Nor will one pleasure stay, tho' he intreat.

" Thus, then, 'tis sure that Virtue's very pains,
" The joys of vicious Pleasure far exceed ;
" While conscious approbation firm sustains,
" The human mind in every time of need.

" By Vice is nearly quench'd bright Virtue's flame,
" Now mortals act not by her blisful rules,
" But are obedient to perverted shame,
" And call her vot'ries silly doating fools."

Here ceas'd the Dame: to shun Sol's scorching heat,
    She in her cell now pensive sate her down,
While from the verdant meads the flocks retreat
    In shady groves to pass the hours of noon.

ELEGY IX.

ON DISCONTENT.

WHAT numerous ills the life of man attend,
    How oft' adown his cheek the briny tears
Steal silently along, while sorrows bend
    His soul to earth, and life a blank appears.

Yet tho' a thousand woes attack mankind,
    Mistaken notions oft' the load augment;
And doubly press upon the anxious mind
    Of him who's rack'd by sullen DISCONTENT.

This fiend is one amid the gloomy train
    Of dire despair, obedient to whose will,
O'er human minds he oft' usurps domain,
    And vex man's bosom with each various ill.

Even Fancy's pencil the foul fiend commands,
  To spread a gloom o'er each gay scene below,
Without a cause he constant sighs demands,
  And rends the breast with unavailing woe.

His cruel hand each tender feeling ends,
  Of mild benevolence and social love,
To self alone his narrow view extends,
  No friendly bliss his slaves shall ever prove.

'Twixt friends and brothers he the brand of hate
  Exulting raises, poisons earthly joy:
Loud strife and anger on his nod await;
  Discord and broils his subjects still annoy.

O mild BENEVOLENCE! still guard my heart,
  Ne'er may this bosom feel his rankling power:
May'st thou soft pleasures to my soul impart,
  And kindly bliss my solitary bower.

ELEGIES.

ELEGY X.

TO SENSIBILITY.

A͟H! what avails it, tho' kind Science ope'
   Her sacred stores to th' enraptur'd mind,
If cruel Care blast every blooming hope,
   In Wisdom bliss nor pleasure will we find.

For cultur'd minds Pain's arrows keenest feel,
   As softest metals deep impressions take,
Or from the water or engraving steel;*
   While harder surfaces its action brake.

What then avails strong Reason's power to ease
   The pangs which wreathe within the tortur'd breast;
Even Friendship vainly then may strive to please,
   Nor can wild Love with wilder grief contest.

'Tis Education points the sting of woe,
   'Tis that makes every feeling more refin'd,
And teaches oft' the briny tear to flow,
   For griefs which touch not the unletter'd mind.

---

* Alluding to the arts of Etching and Engraving.

Ye generous few, say, would ye then forego
 The joy-mix'd anguish of the feeling heart,
Or lose the rapture Pity gives to woe,
 For the vile pleasures sense could e'er impart.

Hail Sensibility! still may my mind
 Thy gentle dictates willingly obey,
Teach me to follow wheresoe'er I find
 Thy impulse lead, and always own thy sway.

ELEGY XI.

ON HUMAN LIFE.

How chearful rose the morning of my youth,
   With airy Fancy's sweetest smile bedeck'd,
Adorn'd with mild benevolence and truth,
   Tho' now on rocky cares my bliss is wreck'd.

Scarce had the morn to riper day resign'd,
   When tempests blast the roses of the dawn,
And plant dire pangs within my tortur'd mind,
   And spread a gloom o'er hill and flowery lawn.

On life's wild ocean launch'd, my little barque
   With wind and sail for Virtue's port still steers,
But, like the innocent and gentle lark,
   She falls by snares which never rous'd her fears.

No vile mistrust e'er enter'd in my mind,
   I ne'er could think that mankind joy'd in ill,
But deem'd their kindred int'rests all were join'd
   The gentle laws of virtue to fulfill.

Thus, without caution, thro' life's tide I steer'd,
  Till dire experience told me I was wrong,
Till vile deceit and violence appear'd,
  Who for my easy virtue were too strong.

By these oppress'd, I with a sigh resign'd,
  Tho' Reason, vainly combating their power,
Fain would have fix'd on other views my mind,
  Fain would have sav'd me till the storm was o'er.

ELEGY XII.

ADDRESSED TO FORTUNE.

With various cares, with various pains opprefs'd,
   Fortune I afk'd, why thus with hand fevere
She check'd the rifing wifhes of my breaft,
   Why thus denied me Pleafure's voice to hear?

" Look round the world," with frowning brow
       fhe faid,
   " Can others boaft of happinefs unmix'd?
" What tho' I grant them all my powerful aid,
   " Are they not ftill with cruel cares perplex'd.

" Think not thy lot is harder than it ought,
   " Thy bread is thine, if for it thou wilt toil,
" And, Oh believe me, it is cheaply bought
   " By Induftry, which ever wears a fmile.

" What tho' in robes of coftly filk array'd,
   " In wanton riot you fhould wafte the day,
" What tho' on fofteft downs your limbs are laid,
   " Yet ftill you know thefe pleafures foon decay.

" But if you calmly to your fate refign,
   " Of happinefs fincere you then may boaft,
" Then fweet Contentment's gentle fmile is thine,
   " Which by no frown of mine was ever loft.

EPISTLES.

EPISTLES.

EPISTLE I.

TO MR ANDREW SHERIFFS, PRINTER.

> While thus I stood, intent to see and hear,
> One came, methought, and whisper'd in my ear,
> " What could thus high thy rash ambition raise?
> " Art thou, fond youth, a candidate for praise?"
> " 'Tis true, said I, not void of hopes I came,
> " For who so fond as youthful bards of fame!
> " But few, alas! the casual blessing boast,
> " So hard to gain, so easy to be lost."   Pope.

Late, Fame began my foolish head to tickle,
I long'd for it as gluttons long for pickle;
Unruly appetite for any food
Denotes the sauce, or else the meat not good.
For Fame athirst, to scribble I begin,
And when once wrote, to print I deem'd no sin.
In magazines, and other publications,
I oft' have read good poems, good orations;

By thefe infpir'd, but chief by mighty Pope,
I fpread my daring wings, elate with hope.

 To Thee, impartial Judge, I firft confign'd
That mournful ditty which firft ftruck my mind.*
Heavens ! with what fearful tremour mute I fate,
While from your lips I heard my effay's fate ;
While you with fmiles benign each error fhew'd,
And on my youthful Mufe your praife beftow'd.
 I next prefent you with Mercator's letter,†
Where I defend our trade from Tim's ill-nature.
Here then you fhew'd me how my genius frail,
Had added to that piece too long a tail.
You fmiling cry'd, " he fure muft be a fool,
Who's not attentive to this certain rule ;
Ne'er with too long a train himfelf to cumber,
Left he have caufe to curfe fuch ufelefs lumber.
Left Satire, with envenom'd teeth, do bite him,
And with the lofs of his dear tail requite him.

---

 * Elegy on the death of Mifs Gordon, being the firft piece the Author had ever written.

 † Some perfon under the fignature of Timothy Mark, took upon him to fatarize the merchants for ftanding in and walking before their own fhop doors. The Author, being a merchant himfelf, defended the honour of the trade in the beft manner he could. This letter, being a profaic compofition, may by fome be thought to be improperly mentioned amidft poetical performances ; but this epiftle recounts to Mr Sherrifs the Author's firft effays, whether in profe or verfe:.
 The Elegy and Letter were both printed in Mr Sherrifs' Magazine.

He may be sure the critics quick will find
This solitary piece which lags behind."
I, thus advised, e'en slip'd away my tail,
And thus the hopes of snarling critics fail.*

Next in heroic verse I rais'd a squabble,
From the Spectator versifi'd a fable:
But mark the end!—my only aim was praise,
And all my pains an odious hiss repays.
Each empty blockhead in the street thus talks;
Lo! where with lofty stride the Poet stalks;
They ask, if such a new-born piece is mine?
And say, you are the fav'rite of the Nine.
Even in the public street, with cruel spite,
They ask what child of mine next views the light:
They of far baser crimes than these accuse me,
And with the horrid name of thief abuse me.
They cry, you'd on us palm another's wit,
Your fable you must own before was writ.

What horrid crime to me as yet unknown,†
Steep'd me in ink's black liquor o'er the crown:

* This tail was a sentence or two very improperly tacked to the letter, of which it had no need, and by which an ill-natured critic could have seized the unfortunate Author, and torn him to pieces at his own leisure.

† I intimate once for all that, as this epistle was written as an imitation of Pope, the reader must not be surprized to find it pretty closely so in some places.

That flood which, as the Poet's whim or spite
Induces him or good or bad to write,
Dips all in black, or brightens all to white.

 Sure, poverty, disgrace, and pain attend,
Those wretches who at Phœbus' altar bend.
Those may be sure who will invoke the Nine,
At their success each empty sot will pine.
With calumny they'll try to blot their fame,
And blast the buding honours of their name.
Yet blockheads jests should never give offence,
If satire comes not from the man of sense.
For here that saying verify'd is found,
The emptier vessel has the greater sound.
Tho' the drone bee, with loudest hum can sing,
Yet are we certain that he wants a sting.
How foolish, then, if from this drone we flee,
Yet bare our bosoms to the armed bee!
Such is their fate, whoe'er they are that write,
The baser passions only to delight;
From Vice and Folly they insure applause,
Who still will praise those that support their cause.
While Virtue, frowning o'er th' unfriendly lay,
Bids infamy the wretches toil repay.

 In one point only to the town I yield,
And vanquish'd in that point I quit the field.
They tell me, for a Poet I'm not fit,
For sure a merchant ne'er was meant a wit.

Better behind the counter I had ply'd
The wav'ring balance, and my friends fupply'd
With goods, for which in ready cafh they pay'd;
While I the rifing heap of gold furvey'd,
With pleafure faw my ftore increafe each day,
And threw my paper, pens, and ink away.
This goodly refolution oft' I've form'd.
But by fome curfed fault 'tis ne'er perform'd:
The Mufe ftill bids me meafur'd verfe indite,
And ftill I'm plagued with a defire to write.
When in the book, intent to place a debtor,
I know not how it is, 'tis fure by Nature,
I write to fuch a man I've fold fuch goods,
Who's broke, and put my mafter in dull moods:
Juft as my honeft Friend, my darling Pope,
Dear foother of my cares, and all my hope,
Tells me a lawyer's fon, tho' dad it crofs,
" Still pens a ftanza, when he fhould engrofs."

Fir'd with the mighty powers of Gray Goofe
    Quill,
My head ftill dictates, and my hands fulfil.
Better, thought I, in idle hours to write,
Than rival youths in love, and raife their fpite,
Sure they can never envy thefe my lays,—
But I forget, each blockhead pants for praife;
And is fo vain at every word, he fwells,
On his imaginary charms he dwells;

Even though at him a whole affembly laugh'd,
He joys, as if delicious praife he quaff'd;
At his odd gait tho' every fellow point,
He thinks he's form'd like Venus in each joint;
Among the Ladies, or among the beaus,
Is he fo happy as to have fome foes;
Is there a coxcomb, emptier than himfelf,
Envies his blifs, it prides the foolifh elf;
If afk'd, what poet wrote a late lampoon,
Whofe praifes echo thro' each ftreet in town?
He fays, you'll think I praife myfelf indeed,
For 'twas a fancy came into my head.

 If fuch as thefe alone diflike my lays,
I'll tell them plain I never wifh'd their praife;
But if one worthy man my verfes blame,
And fay they're wrote with an improper aim;
If Innocence or Virtue blufh to hear
My lines, or one foft Virgin drop a tear;
By them impell'd, thefe cenfures fhall condemn
My works to perifh by devouring flame.

 Even while my friends, with an obfequious care,
For me the penfion of a clerk prepare,
I fcribble on, and wifh fuccefs and joy,
While they for me their anxious cares employ.
And conftantly this precept grates mine ear,
A carelefs man to beggary draws near.

If they fucceed, I fhall be happy ftill,
For well it feems they know I love a quill.

  As Archane in fome corner fpins his thread,
Not to be deem'd an artift, but for bread,
So, tir'd at laft, I empty praife difclaim,
Nor longer wifh to dignify my name.
In fecret now myfelf alone to pleafe,
I often rhyme away my hours of eafe ;
But find the Mufes gain new ground each day,
That ends in work which but began in play.

EPISTLE II.

TO MR GEORGE CRUDEN AT OLD-DEER.

INTRODUCTION.

Here, dearest George, I send a fiction,
Not over nice I own in diction,
But if it serve to pass an hour,
I'll bless the Muses friendly power,
Which gave me skill to form a lay,
Could chase the envious spleen away,
Both from myself and from my friend,
Which here I vow is all my end.

Oft' Avarice is cheated of its aim,
And ev'n Frugality we sometimes blame:
Such was my fate: long had I sigh'd for Pope,
But when the best edition crown'd my hope,
A sixpence sav'd did all his charms efface,
And mark'd him, spite of Bell, with foul disgrace.
The dire offence his lifeless shade awoke,
And thus his frontispiece enraged spoke.

" How dar'st thou, wretch, for me profess re-
    gard,
Yet thus insulted see your fav'rite Bard;
Ah! what avails the pious care of Bell,
Who toil'd to have my writings printed well:
If thus a bungling bookbinder disgrace
My sacred page, and ruin my best face.
So hideous am I, I scarce know myself,
But let me never rest upon thy shelf;
Till purifi'd, at least, in some degree,
The best edition of my works I see;
Else, by my dreadful Dunciad now I swear,
Thou and thy race shall feel continu'd fear
Of hateful duns, of prison's opening gate,
And all those terrors bankruptcy await:
With fearful visions shalt thou be distress'd,
Nor ever with thy wonted sleep be blest.
Till from my face are wip'd those marks of shame,
In fair gold letters 'till I read my name:
As for my coat, I will contented bear it,
Till I with decency no more can wear it;
Then for a new one I will trust your love,
But I must choose the taylor, next, by Jove;
Nay, more, Sir, I will none of your coarse stuff,
As if 'twere winter, and I cloath'd in buff.
If these commands you peevishly refuse,
Then I shall instantly arrest your muse.

By me unaided, write, if write you can,
By me who taught you even the art to scan.
How will you rage when I shall seize your lyre,
How dumb you'll be when I no more inspire.
In vain you'll gnaw your pen, and try to write;
In vain with senseless rage your lip you'll bite.
In vain the partial God of verse accuse,
At my request he shall withhold the Muse.
For by these presents, let all mankind know it,
Phœbus has crown'd me Prince of every Poet.
Ah! think not then I'll e'er allow my lays
Thus to be bound, like awkward girl in stays.
Attend to what I say, and do my will,
So shall the Muse and I assist you still.
Quickly obey, and by your good behaviour,
Secure my aid, and great Apollo's favour."
Here paus'd the Shade.—With grief and shame
    I sigh'd,
And trembling, thus I to great POPE reply'd:
" O! ever lov'd, O! ever honour'd shade!
Fear not, thy rites of binding shall be paid;
My care shall bid new beauties deck thy face,
And quickly wipe away thy late disgrace.
What tho' a dunce, like Cibber, dim'd thy rays,
See friendly Dalachy thy loss repays;
His golden letters shall the gloom dispell,
And thou shalt love him as thy patron Bell.

But ah! avert thy sacred rage from me,
Smooth thy dread brow, nor longer let me see
Those awful frowns lower o'er thy late gay face,
Resume thy smiles, recall thy every grace;
And on thy humble subject bend thine eyes,
With milder look, and bid his joys arise.
So shall the Muse, by thy sweet smile inspir'd,
Praise, as she can, the bard she much admir'd..
O'er thy dread tomb she'll hang a pensive lay,
A grateful tribute to thy name she'll pay;
She'll in thy praise expend her latest breath,
Nor e'er the theme resign, till forc'd by Death."
The Shade seem'd pleas'd,—And thus resum'd
 again:
" Nor of thy recompence shalt thou complain.
Hear, while I tell what subjects fit the Muse,
And what, as worthless, she should still refuse.
Since first her heavenly voice on earth was heard,
Since on the mind her influence appear'd;
Since mighty Homer strung his epic lyre;
And Pinder, careless, struck the tuneful wire.
In verse (as every thing) we still may see,
How Poets about trifles disagree.
As shallow wits the solid substance pass,
T' admire the shadow on reflecting-glass.
So critics leave the meaning of a song,
To judge if rhyme or verse be right or wrong.

The empty form to latent sense prefer,
Nor blame an author, tho' his judgment err.
Faults in the verse with them alone are crimes,
He gains their favour who best clinks his rhymes.
With spleen some critics even my works survey,
Because to rhyme I mould my moral lay.
Whilst some my rhyme to Milton's verse prefer,
Those say I'm best, and these, I'm worst, aver.
But leave this wrangling crowd, and now survey,
Where MILTON, YOUNG, and THOMSON, form the lay.
These three, the fathers of blank verse appear,
And I their pleasing Muse with transport hear.
Great MILTON's head even God himself has grac'd,
And on his brows unfading laurels plac'd;
While he the deeds of waring angels sings,
Around him listening seraphs clap their wings;
And while his genius paints how Satan fell,
Attention follows even to dreary Hell.
By angels circl'd, and by angels prais'd,
See YOUNG's above each poet's name is rais'd;
See Immortality his temples crown,
And at his feet lay all her glories down;
See, how a heavenly smile invests his face,
Whilst wreaths of Aramanth' his temples grace.
Such are the laurels Virtue gives the bard
Who's friendly to her cause; her bright reward

Beyond the narrow bound of time extends,
And into happier worlds her friends attends.
   See where sweet THOMSON tunes his charming lyre,
Whom all the beauties of the year inspire;
Reason and Decency correct his rage;
Not nicest Modesty dare blame his page.
Nature and strict morality conjoin'd,
Shew that the man and poet shar'd his mind.
Still keep his path, and be your views the same,
To please the good and virtuous your aim.
So shall bright Virtue, spite of Envy's frown,
Crown you with praise, and make her fame your own."

EPISTLE III.

TO MR JOHN MOIR, PRINTER, EDINBURGH.

Oh! Moir, to thee a wretched bard complains,
To thee, 'tis all he has, he gives these strains!
If verses would but pay what poets owe,
The scribbling tribe no want of cash could know.
Since paper credit oils the wheels of trade,
Why should not we by writing gain our bread?
If every verse of genuine worth but gave
A single shilling to the Muses slave;
Then would the prison ope' her iron gate,
And yield full many a bard to rooms of state.
But different, far, alas! we write for you!
The empty laurel only binds our brow.
To want expos'd, and pinch'd by dire disease,
We meet the fate of all who dare to please.
Of all who fir'd by genius of the muse,
Each gift but fame, from fortune's hand refuse.
 Tho' I, with unambitious sober aim,
The Muse invoke, without a wish for fame;
Yet, unexempted from the poets fate,
Th' effect I feel of giddy fortune's hate.

Crofs'd in each plan by too fevere a doom,
Already forrow nips my youthful bloom.
Tho' fcarcely ripen'd into perfect man,
Mine eyes with tears are dim, my cheeks are wan.
Relentlefs grief my drooping foul invades,
And every profpect with a gloom o'erfhades.
Tho' gentle hope my former cares beguil'd,
And after fcenes with unborn pleafure fmil'd.
Yet now defrauded of that precious ftore,
Of future happinefs I hope no more.
With no gay fcenes of elegance and eafe
My fancy teems, far humbler wifhes pleafe.
In calm retirement now I hope to gain
A life from pleafure free, exempt from pain.
There, in the vale of Science and of eafe,
My vacant hours the heavenly Mufe fhall pleafe.
She fhall my forrows footh, decreafe my toil,
And teach me at life's little cares to fmile;
Teach me content, and virtue ftill to prize,
And the mean arts of Mammon's fons defpife.
To mild Philofophy directs my view,
And bids me Reafon's dictates ftill purfue:
Tells me that riches happinefs deftroy,
And that content 's the only lafting joy.
What tho' the gifts of fortune may confer
An outward pomp, fhall we a fhew prefer
Before the folid pleafure Virtue gives,
From which the mind a fteady aid receives?

Tho' Nature fail, and tho' the seasons cease,
The soul which Virtue rules retains its peace.

 From East, from West, tho' various treasures flow,
Shield they their owner from the shafts of woe?
Behold the man of greatest wealth possess'd,
Say, Muse, is not this wealthy person bless'd?
Has he a wish unsatisfied, which can
Lodge in the bosom of still restless man!
See, on his nod a numerous train await?
See, how his table groans 'neath loads of plate?
The gilded chariot ready waits his call,
And art exhausts her treasures on his hall;
Yet, without rest, on beds of down he lyes,
While from his bosom burst unceasing sighs.
" Insulting fortune, what is all thy store,
My soul, unsatisfi'd, still calls for more?"
Thus he complains,—" not all my wealth can buy
The blissful ease of him who heaves no sigh,
Whose features wear the smile of sweet content;
Whose peace is guarded by a life well spent."
 But, different far his humble peaceful lot,
Whose wealth occasions no uneasy thought,
Unvex'd by riches, luxury, or ease,
Who rises happy, and who sleeps in peace;
Who calmly steals along the vale of life;
Who shuns wild fortune's gifts, and passion's strife;

Who Virtue loves, where'er he her behold,
In rags attir'd, or when adorn'd with gold;
Who to life's vale with pleasure can subside,
Tho' bless'd by Fortune, who restrains his pride,
Unmov'd, who listens to the voice of praise,
And, with a frown, smooth flattery surveys.

Such is the life I fondly hope to lead,
And such the pleasing path I wish to tread;
Calm and serene, to pass each happy day,
And soothe each sorrow with some plaintive lay.
Life's bustle suits not with the views which heaven
To me for other purposes has given.
Some rural seat is all I wish to find,
Safe in its shade from vice to screen my mind.
Which, tho' it virtue loves, and can compare
Evil with good, pines in life's public glare,
And fearful shrinks into retirement's shade,
Its fainting courage and its strength to aid.
There, safe from flattery, vanity, and vice,
I calmly weigh, and reasonably choice.
There to my books, as to my friends, I fly,
Those spotless mirrors where truth meets mine
      eye:
There, unadorn'd, I men and things behold,
Stript of the varnish of deceitful gold.
There, virtue's heavenly beauties meet my view,
Nor can vice hide the horrors of her brow.

Unbias'd judgement there performs her part,
And gives to Virtue all my yielding heart.
  Next, let us view the scenes of public life,
Mid noise, and bus'ness, and wild passion's strife;
The soul confounded, losing all her power,
Meanly obeys the tyrant of an hour;
Forgets mild virtue, and rejects her sway,
Tho' conscience leads, and reason points the way.
And wandering devious takes the downward road,
To pain and misery's darksome dire abode;
Where, lash'd with thorns, repentance vainly
    groans;
Where headstrong folly her rash steps bemoans.
Where fruitless tears, tho' ever doom'd to flow,
Will never ease the wretch's endless woe.
Far better, then, from such dire ills to fly,
And wisely shun our danger e'er we die.
  But here, my friend, methinks you cry, "enough
Of lifeless rhymes, cramm'd up with moral stuff.
If you would have me read, add fancy's fire,
Or ne'er again presume to touch the lyre.
Can such a letter serve to entertain
A vacant hour? where still I search in vain
For something sprightly, or for something new,
Instead of which, dry morals meet my view.
See, in its front, the prison's iron door,
Where clanking chains, and reeling drunkards
    roar.

Its dreadful end I am afraid to tell,
Thy letter, friend, already is in hell.
Next, then, behold the rising flames aspire,
And, see, thy rhymes dissolv'd in floods of fire."
This said, forgetting friendship's sacred name,
Urg'd by the spleen, my letter feeds the flame.
Hold yet a moment, hold your thoughtless hand,
Its fate respite, remove the fiery brand:
It yet may please, it yet may cause you smile,
Thus would you stigmatize my friendly toil.
So much respect you owe an humble friend,
At least to hear him till he makes an end.
Nor then should fury guide, nor headstrong will,
The sentence you pronounce, be't good or ill.
For mercy even our enemies deserve,
Let mercy, then, tho' worthless, me preserve;
Beneath its covert I my shelter take,
And hope you'll spare for sacred friendship's sake,
Which in my breast to thee will ever glow,
Yet ne'er can pay the favours which I owe.

When in a serious mood, some after time,
Keep and peruse this scrawl of moral rhyme;
It then may please, tho' now it grates your ear,
Then you'll with calmness and with candour hear.
Then you'll commend, tho' now you chance to blame,
And bliss the writer with a friend's dear name.

EPISTLE IV.

TO MR JOHN BELL,

BRITISH LIBRARY, STRAND, LONDON.

Patron of learning, and the Muse's friend,
To thee this tributary lay I send;
I long expected some great bard would dare
The arduous task, thy merits to declare:
But, or ingratitude prevents their lay,
Or inattention steals thy praise away.
Unbrib'd by int'rest, fearless and sincere,
I point the pen in hopes you'll kindly hear
A youthful Muse, whom no ambition guides,
O'er whose plain numbers flatt'ry ne'er presides;
Who knows that virtue rules her honest soul,
While warm within, she feels her impulse roll,
That impulse still she follows, nor exceeds;
Parnassus' flowery paths she cautious treads,
Fearful, each shining action she surveys,
Which, if not vicious, justly claims her praise.
Thy toils her willing gratitude demand,
Thou merit'st well this tribute from her hand;
Gladly she gives, then sure you'll not refuse
The commendation of an humble Muse,

To fame unknown, who fearful spreads her wing,
And dares alone, when virtue prompts to sing.
Weak is her genius, and her powers but small,
Yet, freely, in thy praise she'll waste them all.
Praise, merit's efforts always should reward,
And 'tis a theme belongs to every bard.

  See, how great SHAKESPERE, by thy labours clear'd,*
Shines forth, anew, as he at first appear'd;
Nay, still more elegant, in him we see,
What future times may yet expect from thee.
  See, in long order, Britain's Bards appear,†
See them the labours of thy love revere.
Behold what joy chears every tuneful shade,
To see their works by thee immortal made,
By thee adorn'd with every winning grace,
In every library they gain a place.
Well did you see, great BELL, and well you knew,
That merit will be courted but by few.
Unless with some external shew adorn'd,
With thoughtless inattention it is scorn'd.
Thy pious care grac'd every bard anew,
And made his works an object of virtue,
Now gaze we on their page with curious eyes,
And still are restless, till we gain the prize.

* His Edition of Shakespere's works.   † His British Poets.

The prize obtain'd, we home exulting bear,
And still admire, and hold for ever dear.

Thy hand collects the Muse's scatter'd strains,*
And saves the smallest of her lov'd remains;
Arranges clearly what confus'dly lay;
Her gold refines, and clears her dross away.
See round sweet ANNA's † lyre fresh garlands hung,
Improve the accents of her charming tongue.
See CRUSCA's † beauties fresher rise to view,
And brighter shine when thus adorn'd by you.
See THALIA ‡ smiling o'er thy great design,
Which bids her graces with fresh lusture shine.
While all the Muses thy protection claim,
Mine fain would honour thee with deathless fame.
But vain her labour, for thy name shall bloom,
When her's is bury'd in oblivion's womb.
By bards unborn thy praises shall be sung,
When the lov'd Muse no more shall prompt my tongue.

Small is the pittance fortune has allow'd,
Small are the favours she on me bestow'd.

* Classical arrangement of fugitive poetry.

† The British Album, or the works of Anna Matilda and De la Crusca.

‡ The Theatre.

Yet, from my fund, small as it is, I take
A weekly tribute for the muse's sake.
Gladly my present bring before her shrine,
Which, tho' but small, with freedom I resign.
If wealth were mine, a worthier gift I'd bring,
And all my genius strain her praise to sing;
Her praise, who can unfailing peace impart,
And chase dull sorrow from the human heart.
Her power the pang of unregarded love
Can gently soothe, or from the mind remove.
Mid solitude with her the bard enjoys
The sweetest converse, and the purest joys.
Tho' friendship fail, and fickle fortune frown,
The Muse's smile these trifling ills shall drown.
Tho' fortune frown, the Muse beguiles my care,
And renders even her frowns the less severe.
What tho' in humble station I am plac'd,
I spurn at wealth, if I'm with virtue grac'd.
A vicious mind, tho' varnish'd o'er with gold,
Each friend to virtue must with scorn behold.
And virtue throws a lustre round the shade,
Which she her happy residence has made.
However humble, or however poor,
She chears, she charms, and blisses every hour.

EPISTLE V.

TO A SOCIETY

WHO REFUSED THE AUTHOR ADMISSION AS A MEMBER.

Farewell, for ever, her deceitful charms,
Science no more shall lull me in her arms.
Convinc'd, tho' late, I from her shrine must fly,
I yet look backward with a tearful eye.
As one who sees, dissolv'd in flames, his dome,
Thro' the wide world with houseless head must
    roam.
So I, who deem'd my labours at an end,
And fortune now at last should prove my friend.
By other means must this new loss supply,
Resolv'd to conquer, or resolv'd to die.
Now Mammon's hand unveils his countless store,
And learning's empty visions please no more.
Adieu! forever, to the Muses hill,
For I have rhym'd, and dream'd, and wrote my
    fill.
Now leave me, Phœbus. let the Muse depart,
Nor with your useless raptures warm my heart,
On golden dreams no more I wish to feed,
But hope to prove th' effect of gold indeed.

Which, even to fools, can merit give, and fame,
Then sure to me it ought to give the same,
Who to the Muse have been a slave too long,
Chain'd by the syren sweetness of her song.

Come, INDUSTRY, to me display thy charms,
Nor let me grasp a phantom in my arms,
Which, like a Premier, promises and pays,
Its gift as empty, as itself is, praise.
Yet 'tis a truth, which to relate I'm griev'd,
Too many bards are by this shade deceiv'd.
Who find, alas! too late that saying true,
Hunger each bard does as his shade pursue.
Of wretched poverty and wit the heirs;
Not only hunger, but contempt is theirs.
Such, even their fate, who write not for a name,
Nor wish to gain the envy'd shout of fame.
Perhaps, amusement only prompts their lays,
Their pen, perhaps, love's dictate but obeys.
Fools that they are! to think wit pleases love;
Each day may such an idle thought remove.
Behold the picture of th' enamour'd wit,
With such a wretch could woman's heart be smit'.
See, how at awful distance still he wooes.
And his lov'd fair one, like her shade, pursues.
Turns where she turns, yet still avoids her reach,
And is, good soul, like it, devoid of speech.

Perhaps a daring fonnet given the maid,
Relates what, could he fpeak, he would have faid;
But then he's fo confounded by her charms,
And in her prefence feels fuch dire alarms,
That reafon foon forgets her rightful fway,
And learns her fubject paffion to obey.
    But whence, my Mufe, can fuch digreffions
           rife,
" Faith, 'tis a doubt with me, (fhe archly crys;)
Unlefs by fuch to praife *Me* you fhould mean,
Who am your miftrefs, and who ftill have been.
What tho' you fwear you now will give me o'er,
Like a poor caft off difregarded w—re.
Yet thefe expreffions, like the empty wind,
Shall pafs, nor leave a fingle tract behind.
Again, you'll court me, as you well muft know,
I aid your joy, and mitigate your woe.
I take the dull inanity away,
Which langour throws o'er every gloomy day."
" But whether now? hold, if you love me, hold,
Tho' I've forfworn you, ftill I'll be fo bold,
As for this once to beg you'd aid my pen,
Againft a lawlefs fet of favage men,
Who've wrong'd me vilely, wrong'd me, I muft
           fay:
Then teach me how this wrong I fhould repay."
Here paus'd I:—and the Mufe again reply'd:
" Your fuit by me, my friend, was ne'er deny'd,

EPISTLES.

Attend, and see my power a scene displays,
Worthy of HOMER's, or of VIRGIL's lays.
Raise then thy voice, my dictates to fulfil,
And while thou sing'st, my power shall aid thee still.

First see that Sage, whose shoulders spread so broad,
He is the President, whose awful nod
The rest obey; see in his hand he rears
A polish'd hammer, while his other bears
An iron sheet, tin'd o'er with curious art,
And stainless, like his pure ingenious heart.

Behold my favourite B**** at ease reclines,
Forming ideas of unwritten lines;
And while his bosom swells, as I inspire,
With transport snatches up the Scottish lyre;
With ease his finger move across the strings,
I give the nod, and instantly he sings.

Next, let your eyes explore yon youthful sage,
Who's animated with an equal rage,
And, like illum'd with my poetic beam,
From turbid cistern pumps a purer stream.
Him, even the monsters of the main obey,
Such is the force of his prevailing lay,
From Greenland seas at his command they come,
And on his nod depends their future doom.
Around the virgin's slender waist to spread;
Resistless charms at his desire are led.

G 2

The pliant whale bones, while, diffolv'd by fire,
The nightly lamps his liquid fat require.
' Two tin-fmiths here, I fee, two grocers there,
The fifth, a clerk, but tho' intent I ftare,
The veil of night two other members fhrowds,
Rapt from my view, and circumfus'd with clouds.
Thefe, then unknown, muft want their fhare of
    fame,
Becaufe, unhappily I want their name."
 Here interrupting on her fpeech I broke,
And thus encourag'd by her fmiles I fpoke :
" Forgive the thought which fure thyfelf infpires,
Forgive my rafhnefs, fecond my defires ;
Tell, O my Mufe, what victims to thee bled,
What prefents to thy awful fhrine were led ;
When firft a grocer gain'd thy facred aid,
And dar'd to call thee his own lovely maid ;
When firft on Pegafus he foar'd fublime,
And wrote, and wonder'd that he wrote in rhyme."
  Laughing, fhe faid, " why check'ft thou my
    career,
The goal, believe me, is not yet too near.
This once I anfwer, left you fhould repine,
But dare no more, for I'll your fuit decline.
 Firft, then, a dozen of the pureft claret,
(Porter I mean) what does the blockhead ftare
Doft think a dozen of dull porter much, (at ?
To be allow'd the facred lyre to touch ?

Some would give dozens of the pureſt wine,
Could they of ſenſe but write a ſingle line.
As girls for plums will kiſſes give, ſo, now,
On me for favours grocers plums beſtow.
The reſt were tedious, needleſs to relate;
Suffice 't to ſay no mortal ſhares my hate.
Tho' ſome 'bove others I will always love,
Who my diſtinguiſh'd favour ſtill ſhall prove.
Such are the Members which this Club compoſe,
Even thoſe I love who can but write in proſe.
For I'm in hopes, when they in proſe run mad,
They'll write in verſe, tho' 't ſhould be e'er ſo
    bad.
And then you know they'll all my ſubjects be,
As much at my devotion as even thee.

  But turn a moment, turn your eyes, and view
This the laſt ſcene I now preſent to you.

  Behold where CHALMERS at his deſk now ſtands,
Culling the letters out with careful hands;
See, at a diſtance two with balls of ink,
Impreſs in paper what our authors think.
Theſe ſent abroad, ſhall ſpread their writers fame,
Thro' many a realm, and wide his praiſe proclaim.
But if the youth ſhall ſlight the injur'd maid,
Who many a night and morn has given him aid;
Then ſhall his baſeneſs meet a juſt return,
And all his toil ſhall be repay'd with ſcorn.

Behold the essays which this club have wrote,
Fresh from the press into the world are brought.
Wide spreads their fame, subscribers throng around,
And friends their praises to the skies resound.
But now they're read, alas! their fame is o'er,
Their day is past, and they can please no more.
Alas! to think their friends with weeping eyes,
Shall see them plac'd beneath hot mutton pyes!
Nay, worse perhaps, in wrappers for his snuff
The author meets his works—O dire rebuff!
Yet such in time is every author's fate,
Why should they mourn it, or impute to hate,
What is the consequence of endless change?
For man's imagination still will range.
No single author, tho' his parts are bright,
Can give a lasting and a pure delight.
Let writers, then, submit, nor mourn the fate
Which must attend them, either soon or late."

EPISTLE VI.

TO DOCTOR BEATTIE,
PROFESSOR OF MORAL PHILOSOPHY, ABERDEEN.

Accept, great BEATTIE, from an humble pen,
Th' effusions of an heart sincere and plain:
Permit my Muse to borrow from thy name
A certain title to immortal fame.
Malice and envy both shall vainly rage,
Their venom ne'er shall reach my shelter'd page.
By Thee secur'd of success, I proceed; (read?
Who would not buy what BEATTIE deign'd to
Nay, more, allow'd a humble bard his claim,
And bade him grace these poems with his name,
Even censure's self, his frowning brow shall
    smooth,
And critics spare the errors of my youth;
Satire herself, when she beholds thy name,
Her pen shall drop, nor dare my works to blame.
  If, then, your goodness such advantage bring,
Your will express—shall I forbear to sing?
Or, fir'd by you, attempt a nobler strain,
If you approve, I shall not toil in vain.

For long, I own, the Muse my mind has charm',d
And oft' my glowing breast with rapture warm'd.
Oft' has she met me at the close of day,
And found me ever willing to obey;
Oft' has she met me at the smiling morn,
And soar'd with me on fancy's pinions born;
Oft' would she prompt the sweetly pleasing lay,
Which did the graces of the fair display;
Oft' would she turn to moral themes my view,
And teach me furious passions to subdue.
Then, o'er the grave of friendship bid me pour
The pious tear, while heaven approv'd the shower.
But now she faints unequal to her theme,
And sinks beneath the splendor of thy name.
Lost and oppress'd by thy superior blaze,
She bids expressive silence speak thy praise.

EPISTLE VII.

TO MISS N———— P———— AT C——N——H.

Troth, Helen, you are much to blame,
Each friend of yours will say the same;
How dare you such a youth reject,
And all his tender vows neglect?
Know you not he has cash, my dear,
Then to your love his title's clear;
For he has left his soul with you,
And has nought but his body now.
Troth, Nelly, if you'll pardon it,
You have, I'm much afraid, his wit;
Which by the vacuum in his brain,
I scarcely think he'll find again.
Let pity soften then your heart,
Some comfort to the youth impart,
Help him his passion to controul,
Lest he should die for love, poor soul.
Bethink thee then, Eve's fairest daughter,
And shun that horrid crime, man-slaughter.
Let not the luckless lad be lost,
Lest you be haunted by his ghost;

Then, sure, so fair a lass as you,
Would never make a vestal vow,
And of all men alike afraid,
Resolve to live and die a maid.

" Sure this man's mad," methinks you cry,
" How should he know this lad and I
Exchang'd a word? how should he know
I either was his friend or foe?
Besides, why middle in the matter,
For C——y why make such a spatter?
May not I be allow'd my choice,
Without being plagu'd with his advice."

I answer thus :—" For friendship's sake,
I in this cause such trouble take;
Fearful, lest by your charms struck dumb,
The lad should to the point ne'er come.
Besides, my friend 's not over clever
Of tongue, nor can he long persevere.
Now, as I well can spare an ell,
And better far my tale can tell,
In his behalf I you address,
Begging you would your frowns repress,
And chear him with a gentle smile,
Which would his tender pangs beguile.
Be kinder, NELLY, I intreat you,
Lest in his anger he should beat you;
'Tho' lovers seldom go so far,
Yet know he is a man of war;

And with his fifts concludes each quarrel,
As foldiers do with their gun barrel.
Therefore, I beg you'd hear a friend,
Left you repent it in the end.
 Here, with kind wifhes, I conclude;
Hoping you'll think my warning good;
If not, excufe this foolifh letter,
When next I write I'll fend a better.

EPISTLE VIII.

TO MR J—— I—————— AT ABERDEEN.

Troth, brother bard, I hold you dear,
Tho' yet indeed 'tis very clear
You nothing of my kindness know,
And deem me neither friend or foe.
Deign then to answer this first letter,
For well I know you write much better.
Bear witness every tuneful line,
Printed in C * * * * * * magazine.
Vainly you hope to be conceal'd,
By your own native light reveal'd.
If, then, my proffer'd love you spurn,
And to these lines make no return,
Well may I grieve to want a friend,
Who could his kind assistance lend,
Who could my untaught Muse correct,
Point out her faults, shew her neglect.
Direct her fancy how to soar,
And teach her judgment to explore
Paths which she never knew before.
Besides, our views seem both the same,
And entertainment all our aim.

EPISTLES.

Taught by the heavenly Muse's power,
Aright to use each vacant hour;
Our leisure wisely to improve,
By means which reason must approve.
Since by the Muse each thought refin'd,
For virtue's sway prepares the mind.
Benevolence and friendship's flame,
And delicacy's softer name
Together join'd, our bosom swell,
And in each Poet's breast still dwell.
Tho' of us there's a meaner race,
Who interest alone embrace,
Who vilely write the times to please,
Who virtue can defame with ease;
With sophistry who fill their rhymes,
Who flatter vice, and varnish crimes.
Who, like the Priests of crafty Rome,
E'er dead, pronounce the sinner's doom;
And if my Lord for pardon pay,
He still may live the *bon ton* way;
But if, too shallow is his purse,
He may be sure to have their curse;
And be forever shut from heaven,
Unless a bribe to them is given.

   Some of these mercenary wits,
With Peers obtain the name of butts;
To whom they serve full many an end;
Sometimes, perhaps, their humble friends.

Sometimes their confidents they are,
And all their bosom secrets share,
And what indeed 's a great deal more,
They sometimes serve to praise a w——re.
Then their dear patron's soul to cheer,
They write a birth day ode each year;
Wherein, his character to save,
They dig dead virtue from her grave;
And as his ancestors were good,
He heirs their virtues with their blood.
  Here, gladly I resign my pen,
Hoping an answer to obtain.

    P. S. Inclosed here to you I send,
A letter to our mutual friend,
Which you will kindly send away,
And quickly to his hand convey.

EPISTLE IX.

TO MR ANDREW IMREY
AT EDINBURGH.

Dear Imrey you'll not sure refuse,
This tribute from a friendly Muse,
Who by the favour of Apollo,
To you has wrote the lines which follow,
    One night, even in the Muse's spite,
I sate me down, resolv'd to write.
" Without her aid," I cry'd, " I'll rhyme,
She sure can't punish my first crime;
Nor call an idle frolic treason,
When I had such an urgent reason.
As is a letter to my friend,
Which I away to-night must send,
Lest the occasion should be lost,
For he would grudge, if sent by post."
Full half an hour wrapt up in thought,
Thro' my dull *cranium* I sought
A good beginning, there I hunted,
For I can gallop when once mounted.
But rhyme and reason both refuse,
To grant me aid, without the Muse.

And after I my brains had rack'd,
I back again to her am pack'd.
Well, then, there's no help but invoke her,
And faith I now muſt gently ſtroak her,
Leſt ſhe ſhould happen to be muddy,
And in her paſſion turn her fuddy,
Well, to begin.—" O dainty dame,
I'm at a loſs faith for your name;
Whate'er you're call'd, pray give me aid,
Whether you ſtrumpet are, or maid.
My reverence for you I confeſs,
If you're a punk, will be ſome leſs;
And by my troth ſome think you are,
Since you each bard's embraces ſhare:
Well, but pray be not offended,
What once is paſt cannot be mended;
Let me intreat you to indite,
As faſt as e'er my hands can write,
For you may ſee 'em in a hurry,
So pray do'nt now begin to worry;
I'll hear your rage another time,
If you'll juſt now but give me rhyme."

 Faith, IMREY, laſſes will be courted;
She ſmil'd, and I proceed, ſupported
By her, and what is more, by fancy,
Who far beyond this world can ſee.
And now, like happy *Fortunatus,*
As antient ſtory does narrate us;

Who, when he long'd for this or that,
Only clap'd on his wishing hat;
Or when he would some tale unravel;
Or when he was amind to travel,
His faithful hat was ready still,
At once his wishes to fulfil;
And what, perhaps, may stagger you,
Would carry him beyond Peru;
And in the twinkling of an eye,
Return him viewless thro' the sky.
Such is the case with me just now,
The Muse and Fancy in my pow;
Altho' I know not yet their drift,
Are just about the scene to shift;
And will exalt me very soon,
Perhaps beyond the sun or moon.
Or else, belike, they'll take a ramble,
To Merlin's cave, upon a bramble.
For as an old and wrinkl'd witch,
Flies thro' the air upon a switch,
So by their magic power can they,
Where'er they please, a man convey.

  Just as I thought, the Muse appear'd,
And in her hand a branch she rear'd,
Cut from the ever blooming bay:
Follow, she said, I lead the way.
Then, having touch'd me with her rod,
Thro' air with fearless feet I trod.

Long having fled, we 'light at laſt,
Upon a barren heathy waſte;
The Muſe her wondrous wand diſplay'd,
And ſtreight appear'd a blooming maid;
Inraptur'd I ſurvey her charms,
And long'd to claſp her in my arms.
When thus ſhe ſaid:—" Is this the youth,
Fam'd for his conſtancy and truth
To your inſpiring power and mine;
Who ever bows before your ſhrine.
Who temperance ſo long has prov'd;
And who contentment ſtill has lov'd.
Who, tho' not curſt with cumbrous wealth,
Enjoys the ſmile of ruddy health.
Who in each vacant leiſure hour,
Invokes thy ever pleaſing power,
To ſoothe the langour of his ſoul,
And paſſion's furious guſts controul?
And has he yet no proof obtain'd,
That he the Muſe's ſmile has gain'd?
Let him then follow to my cave,
Where he'll a ſign'd diploma have,
That he the Muſes friend has been;
Tho' that indeed is clearly ſeen
In his rough beard, unpowder'd hair,
And his beſt coat, which is thread bare".
Thus having ſaid, ſhe walk'd before,
And op'd for us her grotto's door.

Here temperance with kindeſt care,
And mild content for us prepare
A ſober, tho' a healthy treat,
Such as our fathers wont to eat.
To furniſh which, no blood ſtain'd knife,
Snatch'd from the faithful ox his life;
When he had gain'd his maſter's bread,
And ſtrung the arm by which he bled;
But milk in ſnowy floods appear'd,
And Scotland's cakes on baſkets rear'd.
When theſe were done, at health's command,
Good cheeſe ſtood ready at our hand.
And fruits of various kinds, with art
Diſpos'd around, form'd our deſert,
With good October then we crown
A foaming cup, to keep all down.
When we had finiſh'd our repaſt,
The diſhes were remov'd with haſte,
With houſehold ſkill in rows diſpos'd,
The meal with grateful thanks we clos'd.
Then health a paper ſcrowl diſplay'd,
And then commands the other maid
Aloud to read what there was wrote,
And bade me with attention note
Each word—She ſaid,—ſhe ceas'd.—Content
Thus then began, while I intent,

In reverend filence heard the maid,
Who with a fteady voice then faid:
    " WE, the attendants ftill of poverty,
And often in the train of poetry,
To all MEN by thefe LETTERS PATENT,
Declare you are a poet latent,
For you can live on bread and water,
And poets never fhould feed fatter.
For if a poet once gets full,
'Tis a fure fign he 's turning dull;
Becaufe the Mufe will ne'er infpire,
A lump of flefh to touch the lyre.
No: fhe is pleas'd to fee the bones,
Jutt thro' the fkin like rugged ftones;
The flefh then ne'er retards the fpirit,
For till half ftarv'd there's few have merit.
    WHEREFORE KNOW ALL MEN, Moir's old devil,
Whom God preferve from future evil,
Having now fcrawl'd fome thoufand verfes,
To clean, perhaps, fome dirty a——s,
Deferves the name of POET well,
For he in temperance does excel.
WHEREFORE we fign this AFFIDAVIT,
Contentment, Health, and Temperance gave it.
To him that like an alewife's licence,
Tho' purchafed at more expence,
May give him power to fcribble on,
While there is earth, or wood, or ftone."

Here ceas'd Content :—With magic ſkill
Then Temperance from the neighbouring rill,
A bowl of pureſt water took,
Mine eyes ſhe ſprinkl'd, and thus ſpoke:
" To thee be future ſcenes diſplay'd,
This fluid thy dim ſight ſhall aid;
And o'er futurity's dark veil,
Shall make thy ſtrengthen'd eyes prevail.
There ſhalt thou ſee, in after times,
What ſhall betide thy darling rhymes.
If thou, by fame's loud trumpet fir'd,
Shalt print, in hopes to be admir'd."
She ceas'd.—Before mine eyes appear'd,
A mighty pile of volumes, rear'd
Above each other in a garret,
Which I with wonder 'gan to ſtare at.
When, lo! who comes? a grocer, ſir,
What! will the villain dare to ſtir
My works? and ſhall the dirty trade,
To which by Fate's decree I'm bred,
Firſt violate my ſacred page?
IMREY, you muſt excuſe my rage,
My paſſion I cannot reſtrain.
Shall then the offspring of my brain,
Tho' for them I've been oft' reprov'd?
Shall then my very beſt belov'd
A grocer's greaſy fingers tear,
And to his ſhop unpuniſh'd bear?

Where, plac'd amid the houshold stuff,
They'll serve, alas! to wrap up snuff.
A bakehouse next attracts mine eyes,
Where 'neath two smoaking mutton pyes,
I saw, O horrid! these same strains,
Wherein my pensive Muse complains.
Of * * * * * * coldness, warm indeed,
Beneath two pyes for platters spread.
Then enter'd to complete my woes,
A pair of barbers, dress'd like beaux;
Who, when the pyes they had secur'd,
My hapless rhymes they next immur'd
Within their pockets, but to mention
How them they us'd Ive no intention.
What need I their disgrace relate,
A slender wit may guess their fate.
With grief I saw those lines defil'd,
To finish which I sore had toil'd.
And, turning quick, I silence broke,
And thus with indignation spoke?
" Alas! I cry'd, is this my fate?
I'll wiser be e'er 'tis too late.
Ne'er shall my works be thus disgrac'd;
Ne'er shall they be in garret plac'd;
Nor e'er appear beneath a pye,
To meet vile scandal's squinting eye.
But in my closet sleep secure,
Where they no rascal's spite endure.

EPISTLES.

Hold, Temp'rance cry'd, be not so rash,
See'st thou that heap of dusty trash?
I look'd.—The offspring of my loins,
Against my hapless works combines.
Those manuscripts I held so dear,
In leaves are scatter'd far and near.
As if my very soul to spite,
They're pipes and candles doom'd to light.
I see my son with careless look,
While from my works a leaf he took;
Without respect to 's father's fame,
Most filthily he us'd the same.
Then frown not, IMREY, at the thought,
Fortune thy Celia's name may blot.
Compell'd by chance, it yet may flirt,
Round some vile sink bedaub'd with d——t.
Nay, even my adored * * * *'s,
Whose form thy Celia's far excels,
In future times may wrap up snuff,
And that, methinks, is bad enough.
Since Fate, then, verse and cash controuls,
Why should we fret and vex our souls?
For what can happen here below,
Where we must many changes know.
Fortune not always wears a frown,
Her freak, perhaps, our wishes crown!
Then let us grasp sure what we have,
And use what she in kindness gave.

Thus to my fate, at laſt reſign'd,
I comforted my anxious mind;
When, ſudden, all the fancy'd ſcene,
Fled from my view as 't ne'er had been.

    P. S. Intentions, IMREY, may be good,
But 'tis by acts they're underſtood;
Which to myſelf comes *appropos*,
As by the ſequel you ſhall know.
I wrote this letter laſt December,
If yet it's date I right remember,
And then I firmly did intend,
To ſend it up to you, my friend;
But as we bards are always heedleſs,
Apologies for us are needleſs,
Wherefore I'll ſay with friendſhip's freedom,
Let thoſe excuſes make that need 'em.

EPISTLE X.

TO MR JAMES RAIT AT ABERDEEN.

Dear James, I am resolv'd to write,
Tho' 't were but out of very spite;
'Twould seem you fear'd, lest, with my rhyme,
I'd take you at some unfit time.
I wish 't may be so most sincerely,
And hope I'll make you smart severely.
May this then catch you 'mid a novel,
And from your fancy may it shove all
The bright ideas you have read,
And jumble them thro'out your head.
R.—Curse on the fellow, is he mad?
I thought he more politeness had
Than vex me now, when, to my thought,
His letter will be dearly bought;
If I take patience but to read it,
Let's see it's length—I somewhat dread it.
He writes expressly but to teaze me,
I'll throw 't aside, tho', if 't don't please me.
For with me 'tis a fixed rule,
To treat him as I'd treat a fool;

K

Who thus dares interrupt my leisure,
Yet for my pains gives me no pleasure.
These poets ne'er are understood,
When they are in their rhyming mood.
F.—Hold, not so fast, you'll catch the spleen,
And that has seldom cured been
By any of the scribbling tribe;
Either for nought, or for a bribe.
Tho' of one ancient bard we read,
Who could have cur'd the spleen, indeed;
For when he tun'd the heavenly lyre,
Even stocks and stones it did inspire.
So that to merry dance they fall,
And dancing so, they form'd the wall
Of Thebes, perish'd now long since,
What wonder, when 't cost no expence.
For how could that be firm and sound,
Which danc'd together with a bound?
Without the aid of lime or mortar,
Or even the shoulder of a porter.
Our modern masons, now-a-days.
Ne'er try to build a house with lays;
Nay, if they sung, 'tis scarcely doubtful,
At music's sound their houses would fall.
For oft' their tropes and metaphors
Turn foolish poets out of doors.
And sometimes even the Muse they curse,
Because she thief-like steals their purse;
And makes them glad their heads to hide,
In garrets high, which shew their pride.

R.—Moſt true, indeed, each poet's proud.
F.—Nay, whiſper that, ſpeak not ſo loud.
R.—But then, they're all extremely poor.
F.—Lower, for heaven's ſake, I'll abjure
All friendſhip with you if you ſpeak ſo.   (ſo.
R.—Your reaſon, Sir. *F.*—It makes me ſneak
This, Orpheus, as I ſaid above,
Who had ſuch ſhare of Phœbus' love;
Many more wonders could have done,
Than animate dull flocks and ſtone.
When lions roar'd, he whip'd his lyre out,
And by its ſound drew all their ire out;
So that, like ſportive kids, they pranc'd,
And round about the poet danc'd.
Some ſay they lov'd him very dearly,
But that does not appear ſo clearly;
Elſe, why ſhould a vile ſerpent bite
His ſpouſe, and ill for good requite.
Had Orpheus been by, I ween,
His harp had cur'd the ſerpent's ſpleen;
And ſav'd his 'Dice's life, tho' ſome doubt,
Whether he would have done 't or not,
As poets rarely love a wife,
Who oft' breeds both expence and ſtrife.
R.—I'll loſe my patience, pray you ſtop,
Is this the end, then, of my hope?
Is this a letter?—If it be,
It was not, ſure, deſign'd for me.

What! tell me Orpheus built a city
And then to be so monstrous witty,
'Bout taming lions, and all that,
What signifies to me such chat.
I never thought my dearest Will
Could ever have been half so dull;
Especially when he wrote to me;
I somewhat doubt if this is he,
Let's see the write, faith I'm not sure—
Compare it with the signature.
Yes, now I think on 't, it is he,
He's alter'd since he cross'd the sea;
Tho' by my faith, it's to the worse,
I'm sorry I am forc'd to curse.
However, Sir, tho' you abuse
My patience, much I'll you excuse.
Proceed. *F.*—To write, do you mean Jack?
Why, then, have at you, for I'll talk,
I warrant you, till you shall tire,
And at my length of tongue admire.
Well, now I really think 'tis time,
To tell you where I live in rhyme:
In Edinburgh my lot is cast,
I'm anchor'd there, I think, at last;
Tho' troth not in a pleasant station,
But much against my inclination.
Nought here conduces to improve
My fixed hate, or change 't to love;

For here I suffer every evil,
And am become a printer's Devil.†
R.—Hold, my dear friend, and pray relate,
What funk you to such abject fate.
F.—Well James, I'll tell the truth; indeed,
It was my own poor silly head,
Which, puff'd up with ideal glory,
Gave credit to an idle story;
And rashly did a wretch believe,
Who basely meant me to decieve.
I left my business, clos'd my shop,
Gave up for fancy'd solid hope;
Left Aberdeen with pride elate,
But found my blunder, tho' too late.
Then round Edina's streets I wander'd,
Where for my folly I was slander'd.
With fruitless toil at last being worn,
Homeward, desponding, I return;
But ship'd again. I backward trode,
Unwillingly the same vile road.
To generous MOIR I then apply'd,
Who, as he could, my wants supply'd;
And to prevent a greater evil,
Gave me the honour'd post of Devil.

And now, I've little more to say,
But just conclude, as best I may;
And as my letter's to a friend,
With Friendship's praise I mean to end.

† The youngest apprentice to a printer is generally termed the *Devil*.
See SWIFT.

Friendship's the balm of stormy life,
It soothes each care, and calms each strife;
And when it takes a softer name,
The passion you will find 's the same.
At least, when 't occupies a mind,
By virtue's power from vice refin'd;
By lust defil'd, tho' love may seem,
Virtue exalts it to esteem,
Which friendship is, tho' then display'd,
Between the lover and his maid.
But when it glows from man to man,
'Tis then it follows reason's plan;
When love and virtue are combin'd,
To pour its influence on the mind,
It makes completely bless'd the friends,
O'er whom its gentle sway extends.
In each extreme of joy and woe,
From friendship solid comforts flow;
By which, tho' rack'd with pain, the mind
To its hard fate may prove resign'd.
And when with joy and pleasure crown'd,
Joy will from friend to friend rebound
With double force, as from the glass,
Reflected light more lustre has.
May friendship then our hearts combine,
And mutual flow from your's to mine;
From mine to yours again return,
That both our hearts alike may burn!

MISCELLANIES.

MISCELLANIES.

ON KNOWLEDGE.

> Were man to live, coeval with the fun,
> The patriarch pupil would be learning ftill.   Young.

Lend me thine aid, O all directing power!
Affift my feeble mind, and guide my thoughts,
O thou who point'ft to virtue's flowery path,
And leadft mankind thro' labyrinths of vice!
Enlighten thou my mind, and gild my fong;
Raife bright ideas in my labouring breaft.—
Point where thy fifter Virtue fmiling ftands,
Her arms extending, to embrace mankind.
Defcend, fair Wifdom, occupy my mind,
And teach me how to fing thy wondrous praife.

  Freed from his fetters, now th' exulting youth
Springs on the world to tafte its promis'd blifs;
With fervent fpirits fir'd, and giddy brain,
Thoughtlefs he plunges 'mid the fcenes of life.
In that gay feafon, when the boiling blood,

And airy fancy lead the mind astray,
The sensual part prevails, and godlike reason
Is lull'd asleep by Pleasure's soothing strain.
Yet oft she whispers in our ears, " Beware,
Nor taste those raptures I can ne'er approve ;
For interdicted joys shall change to pains,
And thro' your throbing heart shoot bitter pangs.'
But these low murmurs, drown'd by riot's din,
Ne'er make impression on the thoughtless youth :
Eager he roves thro' each new scene of joy,
Ne'er satiated, still yawning still for more,
Still sighing, still enjoying, still unbless'd.
Hope, with a steady eye, expecting stands,
From present bad foreboding future good.
At last Experience comes, with sour distrust :
These tell him, that those vanities of life
Are far unworthy an immortal soul :
Added to these, the flight of forty years
His mounting blood has cool'd, himself he sees
Just in the jaws of ruin and despair,
And shudders at the dangers he has 'scap'd.
As some base villain, shelter'd in the guise
Of well dissembl'd friendship, stabs our peace ;
Or as the lion, rushing from his den,
Midst unexpecting flocks destruction spreads.
So specious joys, mask'd in a fair disguise,
When knowledge strips them of their gaudy shew,

Shall turn, and sting with treble rage our hearts,
As, less expected, more severe the blow.
  Whether with sentimental eye we view
The sports of childhood, or the scenes of youth;
Or when ripe manhood, chear'd by Reason's ray,
Spreads full perfection, like the summer sun;
Or when with feeble tottering steps we tread,
And the long lapse of eighty rolling years
Has crown'd our reverend heads with hoary grey,
Unstrung our sinews, weaken'd every power,
Darken'd the sparkling glories of our eye,
And scarce our feeble jaws perform their task.—
Even when the flight of eighty years is past,
They find us children, and they leave us so;
And when swift time has silver'd all our hairs,
Half Knowledge' mighty page remains unread.
  Lull'd in his cradle, by th' officious nurse,
The child sleeps sound, nor heeds the cares of life,
And when the hours of soft repose are o'er,
Some gaudy play thing chears his infant mind,
And raises dimpl'd smiles upon his cheek.
Now, by degrees, he mounts to ardent youth,
When boiling blood and passion urge him on,
And pleasure lures him to her soft embrace.
Young reason sleeps, as yet thought immature,
Buried in fancy's maze, forgets her power,
And slumbers on the down of sensual bliss.

Chief, smiling Love, and laurel'd Fame, allure
Youth's giddy mind: on these they furious rush,
Unthinking of the dangers must be past,
E'er they can gain the soft embrace of love,
Or wear the laurel crown Apollo gives.
For these too oft' we forfeit sweet repose,
The one disdain, pride, modesty refuse;
The other seldom is true merit's prize. (clime,
    Say, heavenly Muse, on what thrice happy
First spread fair Science her enlivening beam?
Dimly at first upon the mind she shines,
Confus'd and clouded like the morning sun;
Like him, when risen, her glory shines confess'd,
O'er every nation shedding light and joy,
And humanizing the wild savage heart:
To all the soft concerns of life she bends
A careful eye, she rules the human soul,
And bids bright order from confusion rise.
    When newly fashion'd from his Maker's hand,
Man, pure and innocent, was plac'd on earth,
By God himself into his mind infus'd
Was all the knowledge which his state requir'd.
But when, by disobedience, he incurr'd
The rage of that all potent hand, which form'd
Not only him but all the universe, (gloom
Scarce could the ray of knowledge pierce the
Which, by foul sin, around the mind was thrown:
Now, thro' the cloud of ignorance he toils,

And seldom finds one steady ray of light,
To guide his painful search in quest of truth.
  Darken'd and clouded by the foolish dreams,
Of superstition's wild fantastic brain;
By slow degrees does heavenly knowledge dawn
On man's enraptur'd mind, and shews him all
The beauteous chain which links the universe;
Connects each different species with the rest,
Affixes bounds to each rough element,,
And of these numerous parts one system makes.
So, in some well pois'd government we see
Nor rich, nor poor, usurp each other's rights;
But all agreeing, form one steady whole,
And each is anxious for the public weal,
Because the public weal promotes his own.
Thus, even Self, the meanest principle
Which ever actuates the human mind,
By the wise conduct of some worthy sage,
Extends beyond the ordinary bounds,
And grasps the bliss of all the human race.
  Where seven mouth'd Nilus from the parched
      hills
Of Ethiopia, pours his slimy flood,
And fertilizes the Egyptian plains,
A people live; in antient times renown'd
For all the finer arts of human life.   (plains,
From their bless'd clime, and from Phenicia's
Greece first receiv'd the softening touch of art;

At whose all potent touch their minds reviv'd,
Unwonted force display'd, and pierc'd the gloom,
The horrid gloom, with ignorance surcharg'd,
Which o'er these darken'd ages sullen hung.
Late, unacquainted with the simplest laws
Which Nature dictates to the human mind,
Like brutes they liv'd, and brutal all their joys.
But when bright Science, on their savage minds,
Pour'd her enlivening beam, and rous'd their powers,
Reason awak'd, exerts his active force,
And with keen energy transpierc'd the cloud
Which dim'd the glories of her heavenly beam;
And, tho' to earth confin'd, her noble light
Soften'd the manners of the barbarous age,
And bade each social virtue rise to view,
And lend a relish to each honest joy.
By her just empire o'er the human mind,
She curbs the fiery passions of mankind,
And polishes the rude barbarian's soul.
 Now from wild rocks see stately cities rise!
See palaces and lofty temples built,
Inrich'd with flaming metals from the mine,
Wrought with the nicest hand of human art.
See the rough rock, by Sculpture's hand subdu'd,
Melts into life—surpriz'd spectators stand,
And view of Science the amazing power!
See where the painter bids the canvas glow,

While from his pencil new creations rife!
Behold, how, by the force of light and shade,
The finish'd landscape rises to the view,
As first from Chaos this bright world arose!
Here, airy Fancy, rul'd by nicest Taste,
Judges of just proportion, scans the whole,
By Art's fix'd rules if beauty may be scan'd.
 Following her sister's steps, the ardent Muse
In her soft numbers paints the rural scene;
Or sings the horrors of the martial field,
Where, cloath'd in blood, the grizly power of
  Death,
Stalks horrible, and *grins a ghastly smile.*
Or else, perhaps, she pens the comic scene,
And, with the pointed lash of satire arm'd,
Scourges each vice and folly from the land;
Of each infectious weed she clears the mind;
Then bids mild Virtue reassume the reins,
And curb each raging passion by her sway.
Next, to the melancholy sounds of woe,
She tunes her lyre, and, touching the soft strings,
She bids each melting eye o'erflow with tears;
Awakes the tender feelings of the soul,
To virtuous deeds, arouses every power,
And calls the tear of generous pity forth.
To other themes, perhaps, she swells her note:
With fix'd attention stand the listening youth,
To mark the various paths where bustling crowds

Mount up the icy rock, where, plac'd on high,
The gilded spires of Fame's bright temple rise.
She shews the prize which worthy merit gains,
And fires the panting youth to brave the toil;
Shews, where, immortal on recording brass,
Or monumental marble, fix'd remain
The fame of antient heroes, now no more,
And baffle the devouring rage of time.
Behold the studious sage informs the youth,
And trains his tender mind to noble deeds;
Delightful task! to rouse the youthful soul,
To point the path where glory may be won,
And shew where laurel'd merit stands on high.
Thro' all the wildering maze to lead the mind,
Where scientific knowledge gradual ope's
Her treasures to the close enquirer's eye.

    Such were the days when Greece in glory shone,
And Liberty her children's hearts inspir'd,
By her encourag'd, Commerce spread her sail,
And dar'd the dangers of the stormy main.
But when the baneful flow of pois'nous wealth,
Still more effectual than the Persian arms,
Beat down the rampart Virtue's toil had rear'd,
And soften'd every mind to sensual joy;
Then Liberty, no more supported, fell,
And servile slaves cring'd to each haughty lord:

Till, by degrees, the mouldering empire funk
Down to the dark abyſs, where now it lies.
  As one who, long far from his darling home
Has devious ſtray'd, ſo I returning find,
After the long excurſion which my ſong
Thro' antient times has made, theſe bleſſings all
Which Science on the human mind confers,
Concenter'd in my native country ſmile,
And make her barren hills appear more fair
Than is the faireſt plain, where Aſian kings,
And ſuperſtition, bear tyrannic ſway.
This is thy gift, fair Liberty, whoſe power
Can bid the barren waſte with verdure ſmile;
Thee, only thee, fair Science courts, and thee
The Muſe ſtill follows with unweari'd toil.
May Britain, ſtill by thy ſweet influence bleſs'd,
Ne'er feel deſpotic power's wide waſting hand;
May ne'er ambition, by her dazling bait,
From thy mild rule allure her ſons to ſtray.
Too much, alas! I fear thy power's unhing'd
By gaudy pleaſure, faſhion's idle dance,
And ſly corruption's ſecret ſapping hand.
  At Freedom's voice arous'd, even now the Gaul
Bids LEWIS tremble on his throne of ſtate;
Around him ſee beſieging citizens
Throw-off reſtraint, and, with tumultuous rage,
The natural privilege of man demand;

M

Their liberty demand ; and, with ſtern ire,
Their vengeance on the fated wretch denounce.
Unjuſt deſpotic ſway who dares ſupport !
With wild unnatural rage, when Britain late
Her thriving children on a foreign ſhore,
With hard oppreſſive hand unjuſtly rul'd—
The politic ſly Frenchman interfer'd.
The raging deep long had Britannia rul'd,
With pining jealouſy her power he view'd ;
By jealouſy, the jaundice of the ſoul,
And policy's contracted ſelfiſh views ;
Againſt Britannia's peace a powerful league
Th' ungrateful Frenchman form'd, whoſe dire
    effect
Tore from her mother's breaſt a darling child.
See, now Fate puniſhes the wretch who dar'd
'Mid friends and brothers ſpread the direful ſeeds
Of diſcord and diſſention—Lo ! his fields,
And thronging cities, now reſound the cries
Of war and death ; and fierce Sedition rears,
Amid his forts and palaces, his creſt.
Of this enough.—Now let me turn mine eyes,
And view the numerous band, whoſe worthy
    hearts
Spread light and knowledge o'er their native land.
    Firſt in the crowd, to my admiring eyes,
Nature and mild religion HARVEY bring.
See, where in contemplation's grove he ſtrays,

Grasp'd in his arms the sacred book appears,
From which true knowledge, true religion, flow.
See, how attentive o'er each valu'd leaf
His eye he casts, then, swift by fancy fir'd,
From nature's volume proves each truth he reads,
And smooths religion with soft pleasure's smile.

  See pleasing ADDISON, whose daily page
Scorns not each seeming trifle to exalt;
Within whose ample mind such various store
Of science, moral truth, and harmless wit,
Were lodg'd. To latest times his works shall give
Full many a useful lesson; and his name
In fix'd remembrance on each worthy heart
Engrav'd shall live; and Britain still shall boast
She in her bosom nurs'd so great a man!

  Fix'd in the solemn mood of serious thought,
Bright Immortality and Reason next
Into my view conduct the worthy YOUNG;
The friend of man. Who, thro' the various paths,
The winding paths of sophistry and vice,
Trac'd infidelity, and chas'd her forth—
As th' unweary'd hound pursues the hare;
Till, forc'd from every covert, spent and tir'd,
She desp'rate yields, and waits the coming death.
Prov'd by our nature, by each passion's course,
Annihilation was a spurious birth,
A monstrous thought unborn, till virtue dies.†

† YOUNG.

Solemn and flow, with sacred laurels crown'd,
And led by seraphs, MILTON next appears;
By heaven inspir'd, our mournful fall he sings
In wondrous verse, unequall'd even by him
Whose song the wrath of Peleus' son displays.

Led by the four who circle heaven and earth,*
In still revolving and still pleasing change,
And guarded by the fair majestic powers
Of steadfast liberty and reason's child †,
See modest THOMSON to my view appears,
Soft, smiling, sweet, and amiably mild
His decent Muse. But see, my favour'd POPE
His voice exalts, and blames my tardy pen,
Which dares so long forget the homage due
To him who fir'd my infant Muse, and bade
The willing numbers wait upon my call.
The best, the greatest praise he can receive,
Or I can give, is his, he was a man.

With various laurels crown'd, see HAYLY comes,
From whose kind Muse flows many a useful rule,
The flights of epic fancy to direct,
And calm the rage into the mind infus'd
By invious spleen, fell foe to human bliss.

To these, Imagination's bard succeeds, (strains,
Whose Muse th' unfetter'd mind for once re-
Describes th' idea, e'er the mind can form
The accents which express it. Far and wide

---

* The Seasons.   † Morality.

Her flight directs, amid the pleasing fields
Of ever blooming fancy, and sublime
In airy regions, guided by the hand
Of powerful Nature, paints the various views
Which actuate the busy mind of man.
　Amid the hemisphere of learning bright,
Some of the stars are these ; but who shall count
The numbers which remain. For me, mine eyes,
Tir'd with the lustre of these brightest few,
To wish'd for slumber close, my willing hand
The lyre resigns, and the o'er-weari'd Muse
Gladly retires, and bids me yield my pen.

DEATH, A POEM.

To dignify the trifles of their brain,
The Muses heavenly aid whilst some invoke;
Be it my task, in solemn verse, to paint
The gloomy horrors which attendant wait
On Death, their king, whose still insatiate scythe,
The young, the gay, the rich, the wise, cuts off.
   Young as I am, my breast has felt the shock
His direful stroke can give; my second sire,
The dear, dear guardian of my infant years,
E'er yet his worth I knew, Death's ruthless arm
Snatch'd from my eager grasp, and ever hid
In the dark recess of the gloomy grave.
   Far, far away, amid the burning plains
Of Florida, while yet a child, my sire
From me, from his lov'd family, retir'd!
But while an Uncle's fondness still remain'd,
Scarce could we feel our loss—Death! cruel
       Death!   (join'd
How could you pierce that heart, where virtue
With mild benevolence, still smil'd to view
The peace, the pleasure, of his fellow men.
But hold, my Muse, the elegiac strain

Departed virtue scorns, her worth is grav'd
Deep in the mem'ry of all human kind.
The pompous column, and the buft, She scorns,
And, conscious of her innate power to please,
For deathless fame leans on herself alone.
 Death, thou'rt the touch-stone of all human
  Virtue!
If, with a cowardly, an unmanly fear
We fly thy stroke, then 'tis, alas! too certain
Some future ill our conscience bids us dread.
But if, with firmness, thy near approach
Unmov'd we can behold; then are we sure
Self-approbation can alone support us
In that dread awful moment! when thy dart
Has pierc'd our panting breast, to separate
These dear companions, who so long have liv'd
In perfect unity, in perfect peace.
Into the grave, as useless lumber, drops
The senseless carcase; and the soul swift wings
Back to her great original, her flight. (turn
 Thro' life's wild scenes where'er I thoughtful
Far as my eye can reach, 'tis tumult all,
And maddest opposition; foe meets foe
With discord dire, and jarring interests clash
Loud as thro' heaven's wide arch the thunders
  roar,
O man! vile man! how long deceiv'd by vice,
With senseless folly wilt thou devious stray,

In paths unpleasing to thy Maker's eye?
Hear how he calls, invites thee to his breast,
And offers endless pleasures to thy grasp.
Thus by his prophets spoke th' Eternal's voice :
" *Come to my bosom, ye who loudly groan*
" *Beneath the burthen which tyrannic sin*
" *Has o'er you whelm'd, behold me ever glad,*
" *The worst, the basest, of your race to save.*"
And shall mankind the gracious offer spurn?
Forbid it, virtue, gratitude, and love!

   Man, youngest child of heaven, full often needs
To feel his father's kind afflictive rod,
Which wounds to heal, as the physician's probe
May pain the patient, while it aids his cure.
Did not afflictions, thro' life's chequerd scene,
Walk with kind hand to warn us of our end;
Man would forget he were to die at all,
And scorn the terrors of the gloomy grave.
Hope, with contracted wing, no more would mount
To the empyrean heaven for endless bliss;
But, stooping, snatch the empty joys of sense,
And quick contracting all her broad desires,
Sit down, contented with the scanty joys
Which the vile empire of the brute confers.

   See the warm youth, even in his rosy bloom,
When mounting blood and passion fire his breast,
Pierc'd by thy dart, drops cold and lifeless down,

And moulders in the murky silent grave.
Behold the beauteous maid, whose rosy cheek
Charms and attracts the roving eye of youth;
While something whispers to her heaving breast,
That Nature gave not her these softening powers.
Her crimson cheek, her ruby lip, in vain.
Even in the moment, when her raptur'd soul
Clings to the bosom of some darling youth,
Death, with one cruel stroke, forever blasts
Love's dawning bliss, and stretches her a corse,
A cold pale corse, amid her weeping friends!

To grasp her much lov'd son, the mother spreads
Her anxious arms,—behold! he faints, he dies!
And stiffens in the cold embrace of death!
See, how to heaven she sorrowing lifts her eyes!
See, how her bosom heaves, thick beats her heart
With anguish, with parental fondness torn!

How vain, how fleeting, are the joys of time!
How idly foolish he who leans upon them
For steady comfort, or for endless bliss!
Behold, at one dire stroke of death's huge scythe,
Fathers and sisters, friends and lovers, fall!

THE BEAUTIES OF DEFORMITY.

Nature, to thee myself I do addrefs!
With humble reverence before thee bend,
And bid thee aid me in the advent'rous fong:
A theme to fame unknown I would purfue—
The beauties of Deformity I fing;
Thofe mental charms which make th' unfeemly
    form
Seem fairer far than is the faireft maid:
For, as unfteady as the changeful moon,
And as uncertain as the doom of fate,
Are all the charms the haughty fair one boafts.
Some dire difeafe, fome accident unlook'd
The faireft earthly form may foon lay wafte,
And plant deformity where beauty fmil'd.
Then let not Uglinefs his fate bemoan,
Nor with a partial tongue curfe Nature's doom,
Which fhap'd him of unwieldy lovelefs form,
With gummy legs and thighs, and fquinting eye.
Let him reflect, that tho' he wants thofe charms
Which ftill attract the roving eye of love,

Yet Science and the Muses woo his heart,
And offer all their treasures to his grasp.
Their unexhausted treasures shall impart
Content and knowledge to his opening mind ;
And friendship shall repay what love denies.
Hear, then, my friends, neglected tho' you are,
And thrown unfinish'd by from Nature's hand ;
Neglect not, therefore, to illume your minds
With knowledge' piercing ray; pure reason's light.
Let virtuous actions give your form the lie,
And shew the beauty of your mental powers.
Tho' monstrous-like your grinning teeth appear ;
Tho' a huge mountain swell upon your back ;
Tho' from the upward line your legs depart,
And o'er your haggar'd visage smiles despair ;
Tho' vulgar fools deem you of flinty heart,
Of black and murderous mind a wizard dire,
And to consuming flames, or hempen death,
Your worthless life consign :—Yet let not this
Discourage your adven'trous mind, to prove,
That even Ugliness may Beauty shame,
And shew more charms than can the fairest maid.
 Let those who're shap'd by nature's nicest hand,
Prepare the mirror to reflect their charms ;
Be it the ugly's care to form their minds,
To court each moral virtue to their breast ;
To hear the call which feeling pity gives,

And taste humanity's ne'er failing bliss.
But left the finer feelings of your mind
Should be fermented by all powerful love,
Guard, guard your bosom 'gainst his rankling dart;
For when he enters, balmy peace shall flee:
For know, the fair, capriciously vain,
Ne'er think you subject to his softening power;
With cruelty they'll tantalize your pangs,
They'll with your anxious sorrows sport themselves,
And laugh at all you promise, all you vow.
The only cure which reason can propose,
The rising sorrows of your mind to calm,
From love to call your anxious thoughts away,
Court friendship, for tho' love his smile denies,
Yet your dear friend, regardless of your form,
With eager grasp shall press you to his heart.
If mid the sons of Folly you should meet,
The pointing finger, or th' upturned lip
Of dire contempt, with equal scorn repress
Their idle jeerings from your quiet breast,
And let not boiling rage your peace molest,
Nor in your mind tormenting passions rouse.

Oft' have I wonder'd, why the gaping crowd
Gaz'd on a certain feature of my make,
And downward cast their eyes, with curious look,
As if enquiring, whether they were form'd

Aright by Nature's hand? The truth is this:
The pillars of my frame, my legs, depart
From the ſtrict perpendicular, and ſtand
Inclin'd a little out to either ſide.
Smile not, my friends, while thus the truth I tell,
Even this ſmall inconſiſtency of form,
Has made me often raging bite my lip.
But now to other thoughts my mind I turn.
My late uncultur'd mind, unworthy deem'd
Of one ſhort fleeting moment's care, tho' now,
As a dry ſponge from every cranny ſucks
The liquid element, ſo now my ſoul
Pants after knowledge with unweari'd toil.
And oft' ſhe curſes Love's inſidious wiles,
Which clog her flight, and, as the meſhy net
Draws from their element the finny race;
So Love from knowledge would my mind allure,
And bid me Folly court, her ſmile to gain.
Her ſmile, how vain to me, if Virtue frown,
And o'er my guilty head her arm extend,
Cloath'd in the terrors of almighty Jove.

 Why do I reaſon thus? why thus diſturb,
The quiet which ſo late my mind poſſeſs'd?
A form like mine the fair can never love;
A form which, all geomatry apart,
The worſt of critics could not lovely call.

 Then let me follow that which wooes my heart,
Let Science and the Muſes' love ſupplant,

And from my bosom chafe his painful joys,
So shall my mind substantial bliss attain,
Nor longer for the substance hunt the shade;
Then calm Content each rankling care shall sooth.
And mild Benevolence my days shall bliss,
And Friendship fold me in his faithful arms.

A PARAPHRASE.

ON

THE BOOK OF JOB.

PART I.

> ———————— O thou my soul inspire,
> Who touch'd Isaiah's hallow'd lips with fire.   POPE.

HAIL! sacred book, with heavenly wisdom
   fraught!
Hail! holy JOB, by sore afflictions taught!
Thee future times revere, and hopeful pour
Thy prayer of patience on th' afflicted hour.
The favour'd East beheld thy shining worth,
And bless'd the hour which smil'd upon thy birth.
His princely wealth more princely virtues grace,
The poor oppress'd were gladen'd by his face;
With wealth and wisdom bless'd beyond com-
   pare,
Seven sons, all graceful, and three daughters, fair,
Rejoic'd his hopes, and crown'd his prosp'rous
   state,
With all which could the human breast elate.

His spacious folds contain seven thousand sheep;
Three thousand camels his large stables keep;
Five hundred yoke of oxen plough'd his field;
Five hundred asses yearly colts did yield;
Even Uza's land than he no greater boasts,
Whose trust repos'd upon the Lord of Hosts.

   His sons, by turns, supply'd the chearful feasts,
While mirth and joy inspire their youthful breasts;
His daughters, too, their brothers feasts adorn,
Which still return'd with each returning morn.
But holy Job, impell'd with pious cares,
Each morn th' atoning sacrifice prepares;
Lest heedless youth, in heat of wine had done
Many offences 'gainst the Holy One.
Thus all his children sanctified he
Before the Lord, each day, continually.
Hail! holy man, beloved of thy God,
Tho' destin'd now a while to bear the rod,
By instigation of our common foe:
But fear not, JOB, no farther can he go
Than is permitted by the Lord, thy friend,
Wherefore, believe, and hold out to the end.
Thy spotless life with envy Satan saw;
Thy strict obedience to God's holy law
Torments his mind; he longs to see thee fall,
To rob thee of thy virtue and thy all;
With this intent, he screens himself within
Th' assembly of the saints, and enters in

Before Jehovah. Whose all searching eye
The foe beheld, and all his dark envy;
And awful ask'd, "Whence cam'st thou, daring foe?"
The fiend reply'd, "from walking to and fro'
Within the earth, thro' many various lands."
"And hast thou then," th' Almighty next demands,
"Hast thou considered my servant JOB,
A purer man inhabits not the globe;
Whose upright soul, attach'd to me alone,
With just disdain each guilty path doth shun."
 Satan, embolden'd, did again reply:
"If JOB doth serve the Lord, 'tis policy
Which actuates him; doth JOB serve thee for nought?
Are not his services all dearly bought?
With blessings which, with lib'ral hand are given,
The fatness of the earth, the dew of heaven.
Thou blessed hast the working of his hand,
His substance is increas'd within the land;
If thou continu'st such unbounded love,
No doubt he will a zealous servant prove.
But now—act the reverse, let sov'reign power
Give Ruin a commission to devour
All that he has, with unresisted sway,
His children, goods, and cattle, in one day;
Then see if he'll integrity embrace?
No: rather he will curse thee to thy face."

O

So spake the subtile enemy, but he,
Th' Omniscient God, beheld his policy;
And did contemn it; for his mighty mind,
Boundless in wisdom, never yet confin'd
The richest tokens of his love and grace
Within the limits and the narrow space
Of worldly greatness. Thou, Almighty Lord!
Who to my soul each comfort dost afford,
Help me to own thy power with pious awe,
To learn the wonders of thy holy law:
On me, the meanest of the human race,
Be pleas'd, O Lord, to pour thy special grace;
That I with Job may be allow'd to see, (me:
Thy heart is kind, even when thou frown'st on
In tribulation then shall I rejoice,
And in the rod shall hear a father's voice.

  Say, now my Muse, what answer the Most High
Was pleas'd to give th' accuser's calumny.
"Go," said th' Almighty Ruler, "thou hast leave,
By my supreme permission, to bereave
Job of his substance, but hear my command,
Upon himself see thou lay'st not thy hand."
Thus much obtain'd, with haughty step he turns
From th' Almighty's presence;—fiercer burns
His rage, than when a hungry wolf at morn
Sees a poor lamb, neglected and forlorn
By those who tend it; eager he descends
The craggy cliff, while in his thought he ends

Its feeble life ; so now, with direst rage,
He goes, the likliest agents to engage
In this attempt. The Sabeans first appear,
Eager for spoil and slaughter; without fear
They fall upon the servants who attend
Job's cattle, and of them soon make an end;
One did escape, when all his brethren fell,
And thus to Job he told the piteous tale :
" While with thy oxen we did plow thy field,
Such joy we had as rural scenes do yield;
Our hearts, unboding of the danger near,
Sudden to our astonish'd eyes appear
The Sabean troops, who on the cattle fell,
And I alone escaped am to tell."
His words were scarcely ended, when arrives
Another servant, who alone survives
A like disaster, he with tears began :
" Behold ! O Job, the only wretched man,
That's left of all thy shepherds or thy flock ;
Which, while we tended, lo ! a dreadful shock
Of fire consum'd them, which from heaven fell,
I 'scap'd alone, who this misfortune tell."
This mournful message scarce was at an end,
When, lo ! another audience does attend ;
His faultering tongue reveal'd like dreadful news
And thus to Job the doleful note renews :

" Ah! Job, no more the pride of all the East
Are now thy camels, or thy houfehold beafts;
Three bands of Chaldeans did befet thy field,
Superior force compelled us to yield;
Thy camels they triumphant bore away,
And all thy fervants with the fword did flay;
Had more efcap'd than I, I'd fure refufe
To bring unto thy ear th' unwelcome news."
Nor had he ended, when a fourth exprefs'd
A lofs which, like a fea, devour'd the reft.
" This day, he faid, thy fons and daughters met,
With numerous fervants they the banquet fet;
Thy own firft born was their bounteous hoft,
But ah! too dear the entertainment coft.
For lo! a whirlwind from the defert blew,
And at one blaft the palace overthrew;
Under whofe ruins all thy fons lie flain,
And of thy fervants I alone remain!"

A PARAPHRASE ON THE BOOK OF JOB.

PART II.

———————Hope, the friend of the diſtreſt,
Came to my aid, and ſooth'd my troubl'd breaſt.

WHEN this o'erwhelming ſpeech was at a cloſe,
Straight from his ſeat afflicted JOB aroſe;
His rev'rend head he ſhav'd, and grieving, tore
The purple robe, which, as a prince, he wore.
With woe o'erwhelm'd, not frantic, but profound
He proſtrate fell, and worſhip'd on the ground.
　Ceaſe, O my ſoul! he cry'd, nor dare complain,
God's ways are juſt, tho' nought with thee remain!
A helpleſs naked infant was I born,
And naked to the earth I ſhall return;
Tho' heaven had preſerv'd to me my ſtore,
I had enjoy'd it but a few days more;
Till death, the leveller of all mankind,
Had call'd me hence, to leave it all behind.

No murmurs, then, shall swell my afflicted soul,
'Tis good for me such tumults to controul,
And chearful yield to what my God thinks fit,
To take all from me, or take me from it;
Pleas'd I resign, thy gracious hand gave all,
Bless'd be that hand, whate'er to me befal.

 Heroic patience! O my soul attend
Th' instructive lesson; reverendly bend
Thy will, like his, to the supreme decree,
And own, what God appoints, is best for thee.
Behold the man whom mighty grace sustains,
Unmov'd beneath the shock of fate remains;
Richer in virtue now the saint appears,
Than in the bloom of his most prosp'rous years.
This Satan saw, and now with shame beheld,
The holy man was master of the field;
Saw all th' effect of his malicious deeds,
Did only break the clods, and kill the weeds;
While heaven-born virtue, like an ever-green,
'Mid wintry storms more verdant still was seen.
One effort more the fiend is bent to try,
Resolv'd the saint shall either yield or die.

 Once more among the sons of God is seen
Th' accuser of the brethren; malice, spleen,
And rage, in dire extremes, torment his breast,
And keep his hellish mind from finding rest.
Th' Omniscient's eye beheld the daring foe,
The dark design, the meditated blow

He wish'd for licence to inflict on one,
Who stood unmov'd 'neath all he yet had done.
With just rebuke the King of Saints began:
" Thou lost to all that's good, thou foe to man,
What new malicious plot now brings thee here?
Why 'mid my children dar'st thou thus appear?
I see thy malice, and thy spite contemn,
Against the best, the most upright of men,
My servant JOB—'gainst whom thy rage is vain,
For still he does his uprightness maintain;
Nor dares to murmur once against my laws,
Tho' he oppressed is without a cause,"
" This sullen patience," cry'd th' insulting foe,
"If thou permit'st, I soon shall overthrow;
He huggs his ease, and while himself is spar'd,
Children or servants' woes he'll ne'er regard;
But visit now himself with grievous pain,
Let neither bone nor flesh untouch'd remain;
Then, if with rev'rence he adore the hand
Which thus afflicts him, and unruffl'd stand
The shock of such a trial, I must then
Own JOB to be the most upright of men:
Yet much I fear, touch'd in this tender place,
Thy boasted saint will curse thee to thy face."

Let sense be silent, reason humbly bow
To thee, superior Faith, which only now,
Directed by th' Almighty's word, can shew
A blessed period to the good man's woe;

Thus patience, faith, and love, by suffering try'd,
Shall shine victorious, and confound thy pride,
Malicious foe! whose rage is all in vain,
Tho' given the utmost limit of thy chain:
The Sov'reign Ruler grants thy last demand,
And solemn says, " my saint is in thy hand;
Inflict those pains thou deem'st the fatal test
Of all the love which glows within his breast;
But spare his life, his life I safely guard,
To keep on earth his bountiful reward."

 Thus flush'd with success, past his utmost view,
Streight on his prey the hellish fury flew;
On JOB's devoted head the baneful pest
Fixes invet'rate; no respite, no rest,
To soothe his anguish, can the suff'rer find,
Or calm the recent sorrows of his mind.
Convuls'd with pain, and loathsome to the view,
O'er all his flesh the fretting ulcers flew;
Unusual terrors seize his aching breast,
His couch no longer brings him wonted rest;
No cordial friend is near to soothe his grief,
Or bring to mind or body wish'd relief.

A PARAPHRASE

ON THE BOOK OF JOB.

PART III.

Durate et vosmet rebus servate secundis.
Endure and conquer, live for better fate.

Amid the ashes, see th' afflicted saint
Now sits him down, with pain and sorrow faint;
Nay, even his wife, who should have brought relief,
By evil counsel but augments his grief;
She bids him curse His great, His mighty Name,
Who made the earth, who fix'd the starry frame;
" By this," she said, " provoke th' Almighty's ire,
Then from these sorrows shalt thou quick expire."
Thus answer'd mild the man belov'd of God:
" Shall we repine beneath a father's rod?
Or doubt of the Almighty's kind regard,
Who has for us heaven's endless joys prepar'd

Shall then our impious voice our God arraign?
Becaufe our lot is not exempt from pain?
How feldom does that gracious hand chaftife,
How often is it ftretch'd mankind to blefs?
Shall then a worm, whofe life is but a day,
With criticifm's eye God's acts furvey?"
Thus fpoke the patient man.   His friends, meanwhile,
Had heard the mifchiefs which to JOB befel;
Each took his way, hoping to bring relief,
At leaft to fhare it, if not eafe his grief,
But fuch a load of pain his body bore,
Their dear, their much lov'd friend, they knew no more.
Seven times the fpace which meafures day and night,
Silent they fate, opprefs'd with fuch a fight.
JOB firft this filence broke, and thus he cry'd:
" How can weak flefh fuch racking pain abide?
Curfe on the day in which I faw the light,
May it be darker than the fhades of night;
Becaufe it gave me not an early tomb;
Becaufe it fhut not up my mother's womb;
Why did the foft'ring paps prevent my death?
Why did the grizly king not fnatch my breath?
O grave! why cam'ft thou not, and open'd wide
Thy mouth, from thefe dire ills my foul to hide?

Then had I rested, calm and quiet been,
And these afflictive days had never seen.
In thy dark bed th' opprefs'd no sorrows feel,
No more obnoxious to the tyrant's steel;
The young, the old, the rich, the poor, are there,
Foes grasp each other, and their hate forbear."

Here ceas'd he; and by turns his friends arose,
If by their counsel they might eafe his woes;
But all mistook, and thought that JOB had done
Some great offence against the Holy One.
Their sharp reproofs do but augment his pains,
And of their conduct loudly he complains.

But now th' Almighty Father from his throne
Beheld afflicted JOB. and heard his moan:
From mid the whirlwind thus the Lord began,
With awful voice! " Appear now like a man;
Fear not, 'tis I, thy God, even the Moft High,
I will demand, and thou shalt make reply.
Say, what prefumptuous men are these, who dare
My ways to fcan, my purposes declare?
Who by their folly darken what is clear,
And 'gainst my providence false witness bear.
But tell, where waft thou when the world I made?
Waft thou then present? did I afk thine aid?
To its dimensions didst thou stretch the line?
Or, did thy word its corner stone confine?

Say, didst thou poise it mid the vacuous air?
Or can thy feeble works with mine compare?
When the gay morning stars together sung,
And light from darkness at my biding sprung.
Declare, who fix'd old Ocean in his bounds?
What bars confine him, or what wall surrounds?
Art thou then able to command the main?
And in their proper bed his waves restrain?
Stretch thy wide thought beyond the starry pole,
And try if thy weak mind can hold the whole
Of my amazing works; o'er plains, o'er hills
Extend thy view, from ocean to the rills
Which water earth; there bird, beast, fish, behold
A thousand various tribes, some speck'd with gold;
Some whose dread front, and threat'ning fiery eyes,
The puny race of man with terror flies.
If, then, the creatures of my hand affright,
Thee, and thy race, who shall withstand my might?"
Here ceas'd th' Almighty. JOB his errors own'd;
Again relenting, God his servant crown'd;
Again, with plenty was his table heap'd;
Again, in ease he liv'd, in ease he sleep'd;
Increase of treasure now th' Almighty shower'd
Upon his saint, he double substance pour'd.
His friends condole him on his former pain,
And wish he sorrow ne'er may know again;

Each gives a princely prefent from his ftore,
Till Job is richer than he was before.
Now doubled flocks his ample fold contains;
Six thoufand camels pafture on his plains;
A thoufand yoke of oxen plow his field;
A thoufand affes yearly colts do yield;
Seven graceful fons he has, three daughters fair,
With whom in all the Eaft might none compare.

A TALE.

Begin, my Muse, Tonsorius claims thy lay,
And bids thy verse his matchless worth display;
Crown with the lustre of bright gold, his name,
And give his virtues to eternal fame.
  Long had he added to the chin new grace,
And blanch'd from black'ning hair each youthful face;
When now in labours of the razor old,
By daily success still he turns more bold;
The hairy harvest to his sickle yields;
His razor mows the crop, and clears the fields;
Nor unrewarded were his toil and pains,
Plenty of gold, his soul's first wish, he gains.
Now, anxious how this cash he should employ,
Till it's dispos'd of he can taste no joy;
The thoughts of robbers even his sleep molest,
And break, in hideous dreams, his balmy rest;
At last, resolv'd to visit Plautus' shrine,
And ask th' assistance of his power divine,
Tonsorius goes, while his best cloaths invest
His person, frugally and neatly drest;

Upon his block a large bob wig he bore,
A grateful off'ring to the god of ore;
And in his hand a paper duly fign'd,
That he no mifchief to his realm defign'd,
Much he revolves, the journey much, the coft,
And much, he fears, his labour will be loft;
Refolv'd, at laft, to rifk, or lofs, or gain,
Into his hand he takes his trufty cane;
His fon behind, his loving wife before,
He gains the threfhold, and he ope's the door;
But e'er his toils and travels are begun,
The careful father thus addrefs'd his fon:
 "ANDREW," he cry'd, " my deareft fon, come here,
To the inftructions of your fire give ear;
Whet well your razors, that from every chin,
They may the hair remove, nor hurt the fkin;
Of that beware, for if with blood they're ftain'd,
By every fool our art fhall be difdain'd;
And if a halfpenny reward your toil,
Still thank the giver, with a gracious fmile;
But if a penny from his pocket come,
Then turn him round, and give his hair a comb:
For effenc'd greafe don't fuffer him to plead,
Nor grudge with flower to whiten all his head.
But if of copper he's perchance devoid,
And in his hand a fixpence is defcry'd,

Round the whole circle of your art then range,
But ne'er affront the gentleman with change;
Freely on him a thousand thanks bestow,
And swear you've made him a most perfect beau.
Cry, please you, sir, to look but in the glass.
His form will please him, if he is an ass;
Nay, tho' he's wise, his vanity will come,
Expell his reason, and possess her room.
When thus he's tickl'd, 'tis your time to say,
Please, sir, to wash my staining suds away;
Then, at his nod, you should obsequious stand,
With bason and with towel in your hand;
Be careful on his cloaths you leave no spot;
Brush clean from powder all his sunday's coat;
Thus he well satisfi'd shall walk away,
And think he service has for all his pay.

 The Muse denies the tedious task to tell,
What toils this modern traveller befel;
Patient he bore them, and still forward press'd,
Nor, till the shrine appear'd, would think of rest.
At last arriv'd, before the god he bow'd,
And thus his errand to the power avow'd:
Here, at thy feet, a mortal skill'd in hairs,
Presents this humble gift his hand now bears;
Its grateful warmth shall sooth thy aged head,
And o'er thy scull a needful umbrage spread.
Thus far I come, thy mighty power to prove,
Hopeful, in my behalf, that power to move;

To teach me how I may improve my store,
Safely to guard it, or to make it more,"
He ceas'd. The god with smiles his suit approv'd,
Then call'd a minister, whom much he lov'd;
" To thee," he said, " this mortal I commit,
Improve his judgment, and refine his wit;
Teach him thy arts, the simple to beguile,
Display each secret, and reveal each wile."
 Instructed thus, Hypocrisy began,
Without reserve, displaying every plan:
"Listen Tonsorius: Is thy judgement slow,
To comprehend the force of outward shew,
And seeming goodness? The attractive grace,
Which may be gain'd by cant and sly grimace?
A seeming saint can vulgar souls deceive,
Still prompt to faith, still eager to believe;
What tho' a few may pierce the slender veil,
These few may have the privilege to rail;
Whilst thou with suff'ring godness may'st observe
How ill these censures thou did'st e'er deserve.
Thus veil'd with Virtue's cloak, be wise in time,
Nor pass, without improvement, all your prime;
Securely cheat, securely spread each snare,
From which advantage you can hope to share;
But these are vague directions, mark me well,
While I thy very wish'd-for plan reveal.

Q

Thou know'ſt a youth, thy nephew, tho' he be,
Kindred and friends are empty names to thee;
Thyſelf, alone, of all the world thou lov'ſt,
If thou to me a truſty ſcholar prov'ſt.
Benevolence is by the world approv'd,
By many really and ſincerely lov'd;
Seem charitable, then, thy nephew take;
From ſtitching table him a merchant make.
Among thy friends diſplay the pious act,
And every feeling of their ſouls attact;
So ſhall their charity increaſe thy ſtock,
For they in crowds around his door ſhall flock:
Be careful of the caſh, but ſtill pretend
Thou doſt ſo only to ſecure thy friend,
Whoſe youth, thou cry'ſt, wants caution to improve
The goods of fortune; therefore, as thy love
His thrift began, thy friendly eye ſhall watch,
To fix his profit, each occaſion catch.
Act thus, and fear not but the cheat will hold,
At leaſt till thou haſt gain'd a little gold;
And when thy profits to the world are ſeen,
Behind a thrifty habit thou may'ſt ſcreen
The ſeeming evil, and the hurt evade,
Which defamation fixes on thy head;
For mankind are ſelf-intereſted ſtill,
And in that cauſe will paliate every ill."

"What thanks, my friend," Tonsorius cry'd,
   "are due,
For theſe kind leſſons I have heard from you;

By equal gifts my gratitude I'll prove,
For your unbounded confidence and love."
" Hold," cry'd Hypocrify, " no gifts I claim,
Believe me, Sir, far other is my aim;
Be faithful to thy friend, and teach mankind,
To own his laws, 'tis all he e'er defign'd."
"Then take my thanks," he faid, " I give my hand
That I fhall careful do what you command;
If my example can enforce your laws,
I'll ne'er be wanting to promote your caufe;
Farewell, my friend, I now muft homeward tread,
My parting bleffings reft upon your head,
Who thus have kindly deign'd to teach my mind
With certainty its utmoft wifh to find."
Thus having faid, TONSORIUS backward turn'd,
With fancy'd wealth while all his bofom burn'd.
And now return'd, his loving fpoufe enquir'd,
If he had fped in what his foul defir'd?
" Yes, I have fped," he cry'd, " and future times
Shall hear my ftory, handed down in rhymes,
Which to remoteft ages fhall convey
My name, immortal, by the Poet's lay."
Thus fpoke TONSORIUS. Now he ftraight pro-
    ceeds
To prove his counfel, by the teft of deeds.
His nephew call'd, with caution firft he trys;
To fee which way his inclination lies,

To sway the youth an easy task he finds,
For interest has its force in youthful minds.
A shop he took, and furnish'd out with wares;
Next, to his friends his pious end declares,
That for his nephew's helpless youth he spent
His cash with joy, and begg'd, his good intent
That they would second, and with friendship aid
The young beginner to augment his trade;
If thus they'd act, he'd take the favour done,
With as much thankfulness as for his son.
A while deceiv'd, a crowd frequents the shop,
Tonsorius gains beyond his utmost hope;
At last th' uncautious youth his state reveal'd,
So long, so closely from the world conceal'd.
Indignant now each customer retires,
And all at once the boasted trade expires.
Tonsorius griev'd, but now his grief was vain,
He shuts the shop, and pockets up his gain.

THE CONQUEST OF VANITY.

As in my room, at eve', I penfive fate,
Mufing o'er all the turns of human fate,
The clock ftruck twelve, with melancholy knell,
And o'er my brain a fudden flumber fell;
Then wild imagination roving flies,
A wondrous fcene prefenting to mine eyes.
Me-thought advanc'd to me with lofty pace
Two female forms of the ætherial race;
Both were in robes of pureft white array'd;
Their rofy cheeks the bloom of youth difplay'd;
Tho' both were charming far above our race,
Each was adorn'd with a peculiar grace.
The firft, in native dignity appear'd,   (rever'd.
Each eye, which view'd her charms, their force
The other, drefs'd in glowing blufhes came,
With downcaft eyes, fhe rais'd a fofter flame.
Around the ftrangers all earth's daughters crowd,
Whom thus the heavenly maid addrefs'd aloud:
" I Virtue am, who from the realms above,
Have now defcended at the fuit of Love
My handmaid Modefty my fteps attends,
Who, in my ftead, each female bofom tends.

She to each virtuous joy your heart directs,
And in your breaſt each latent vice detects;
Exerts her power to bend each female ſoul,
And the wild ſallies of your minds controul.
Late, Venus' ſmiling boy, from Cypria's grove,
Wing'd his ſwift flight unto the realms above,
Arriv'd to me, he did his griefs diſcloſe,
And pour'd into my boſom all his woes.
Thus ſpoke the God. " You know, Almighty Jove,
Who heads the ſenate of the gods above,
Gave me the empire o'er each female heart,
Which I maintain, by this all-potent dart.
But, late arriv'd on earth, two direful foes
Diſpute my rule, and break my ſoft repoſe;
With wild ideas fill each female mind,
Which our united power before confin'd.
Your awful charms temper'd my ardent fire,
For you the nobleſt paſſion can inſpire;
But my weak flame, by vice is oft' defil'd,
And by the outward form I'm oft' beguil'd;
'Tis my requeſt you will to earth deſcend,
And in my cauſe with Vanity contend."
" Much I diſtruſt your faithleſs words, I ſaid,
At this a red'ning bluſh his face o'erſpread;
But I will try what yet my charms can do,
Tho' I have been unus'd for aught to ſue.
Then hear me, Daughters of Mankind, attend
For once, take counſel from a faithful friend;

Say, is there ought in all the pomp of shew
Can on a wrinkled face one charm bestow?
Shall aged maidens hop like youthful squirrels,
And totter thro' the town like wanton girls?
With toothless gums, and paint beplaster'd face,
Affect the youthful smile, the pert grimace;
What wonder, then, if Flavia scorns her aunt,
Who, at the age of sixty, is a rant;
Boasts her warm blood, and crys, I'm living still,
And tho' the power is gone, she has the will.
Say, does a lady's bosom seem more fair,
All naked, swelling to th' inclement air.
Or, when conceal'd by modest lawns, it lies
Veil'd from the gaze of rude licentious eyes?
Force ye not Nature, take what course ye will,
The stubborn goddess will resist you still;
Say, will you then a certain good refuse,
And in its stead a certain evil chuse?
Be rul'd by Modesty, espouse my cause,
Submit to me, and own just Nature's laws;
Or else, o'erpower'd by yonder gaudy dame,
You lose your Virtue, lose your spotless fame,
And justly sink to ruin and to shame."

 Scarce had she ended, when an airy maid,
In all the gaudy shew of dress array'd,
Approach'd the gazing multitude, and cry'd:
" How can you make that silly fool your guide,

To rugged toil, and endlefs dangers bred?
She with her empty prate will turn your head,
But follow me, I lead to other fcenes,
'Tis I can bring you to thofe happy plains,
Which fhe, vain thing, has promifed to do;
There, on you all I'll happinefs beftow;
There, there, my empire lies, and there I rule;
Then, will you follow me, or that vain fool?
O'er all the fpacious world I bear command,
And o'er each female mind in every land."
Here plaufive fhouts re-echo'd to the fkies,
Which Virtue only anfwer'd by her fighs;
Some few of all the num'rous crowd remain'd
To her juft caufe by common fenfe retain'd.

ON INTEMPERANCE.

O Virtue, heavenly-fair, where art thou fled,
Where doft thou hide thy melancholy head?
While thy rank foes degenerate man infpire,
With bafeft paffions they his bofom fire;
While Luft and Luxury the world command,
And fpread their bane o'er all our withering land.
No more thy will man's alter'd bofom fways,
But fenfual pleafure he alone obeys.
No more thy dictates pure his mind controul,
And calm the raging tempeft of his foul;
But Senfe and Luxury their charms unite,
And to their banquet, to their bed invite.
Lur'd by their outward form, their pleafing guft,
He fears not in their arms his foul to truft;
Till thro' his weaken'd nerves their poifon flies,
And, like a blafted plant, too foon he dies.
Snatch'd from the world, in youth's full bloom,
    away,
His manly limbs, his once ftrong nerves decay.
To Virtue loft, the brute alone remains,
Campell'd to fmile, amid a load of pains;

While fierceſt rage and paſſion rend his ſoul,
Compell'd the dreadful tumult to controul ;
Compell'd with artificial ſmiles to ſcreen,
The dread, the horror, of the inward ſcene,
Where hope, deſpair, and ſenſe, with diſcord dire,
His boiling feveriſh blood with fury fire.

 Bright Virtue aid me, and my breaſt inſpire,
While in thy cauſe I tune my willing lyre ;
While I the downward ſliding path diſplay,
Where Senſe allures, and Paſſion points the way.
How few the number of the wealthy good,
Who have the ſnares of Luxury withſtood !
How few, what wealth confers, do not adore,
And worſhip Pleaſure, tho' ſhe is a whore !
How few, thy cravings, Appetite, repreſs,
And know, that death attends upon exceſs ;
How few thy dictates, Temperance, attend,
Tho', ſure, thy rules to peace and pleaſure tend,
On life's wild ocean toſs'd, the tender youth
With uncorrupted heart ſtill ſighs for truth ;
Sighs ſtill to find degenerate mankind chaſe
The empty ſmiles on Pleaſure's changeful face ;
Mourns that ſuch trifles charm the human mind,
While Virtue, Wiſdom, both are left behind.
Thus, while untainted, his young mind remains,
Of man's erroneous conduct he complains ;
At laſt, example ſlowly moulds his ſoul,
Then ſenſual pleaſure finds no more controul ;

Loud Will rebels within his raging breaſt,
Still leans to Senſe the more, as more repreſt ;
He now thinks Virtue a mere empty name,
And laughs at that which was before his aim ;
Self approbation he no more enjoys,
But follows with the crowd their baneful joys,
Whilſt immature, pale age, diſeaſes dire,
To blaſt his blooming youthful form conſpire.
In this late age bright Virtue takes his ſtand,
Upon the fartheſt confines of our land ;
And, with a longing, lingering look, complains
That ſhe is forc'd to leave earth's darling plains;
While, in her ſtead, advancing hand in hand,
Faſhion and Luxury uſurp command ;
Behold what dæmons in their train appear !
See what a horrid company draws near !
And, as ſagacious vultures from afar,
Ruſh to the dreadful plain, where bloody war
Unto their greedy maws prepares the prey ;
They, pleas'd, the riſing heap of dead ſurvey.
So, near the throne of Luxury, rejoice
In man's ſure ruin, pale Diſeaſe, and Vice ;
Fierce appetites within his breaſt they rouſe,
They bid the drunkard o'er his bowl carouſe.
When thus reduc'd and humbl'd all his ſoul,
When ſenſe no more feels Reaſon's ſtern controul,

Then in his bosom rages fierce desire,
Then, then, he feels vile lust's increasing fire;
With raging appetite he grasps the feast,
Which gives him all the raptures of the beast.

 Would you the active soul in fat entomb,
And bury reason in a swelling womb?
With Hullio wish the nicest pork to eat.
And at each table fill the largest seat;
Eat, till your belly swell'd to monstrous size,
With portly bulk the gaping crowd surprize;
Just like a mayor, rose from city feast,
You measure round the waist two yards at least;
Then let me hear you reason, if you can;
Then let me see you form one proper plan;
Your soul succumbs beneath a load of flesh,
And dwells, enraptur'd, on some luscious dish;
All other things, as trifles, still she holds,
And in her arms her dearest hog she folds.
You hold the maxim, " 'Tis to eat I live,
Meat, meat alone to me can pleasure give;
Away with reason, and her idle toys,
A modern feast my soul alone enjoys;
What tho' they tell me I invite much woe,
In gout and cramp to dislocate my toe;
An hackney coach will bear my greatest weight,
Tho' my weak limbs can't carry such a freight."

LUXURY AND AVARICE. A FABLE.

VERSIFIED FROM THE SPECTATOR, VOL I. NUM. 55

Two cruel tyrants waged moral war,
Againſt each other rueful arms they bare;
Contending fierce upon the hoſtile plain,
Which ſhould the long conteſted prize obtain;
For univerſal ſway they mutual rag'd,
Nor could their horrid fury be aſſuag'd;
Mirth, Pomp, and Faſhion, LUXURY attend,
Pleaſure and Plenty their aſſiſtance lend.
Five fierce commanders, AVARICE obey,
Beneath their lord they bear tyrannic ſway;
Loud Hunger, painful Induſtry, and Care,
Pale and diſorder'd Watchfulneſs was there,
And tatter'd Poverty his counſels ſway'd,
Plenty's perſuaſions Luxury obey'd; (roaſt.
Theſe two, like PITT or CROMWELL, rul'd the
Full oft they counſel'd to their maſter's coſt.
'Twixt theſe divided, fought the human race,
And fathers met their ſons with ireful face;
By rage and diſcord, weapons were ſupply'd,
With ſtools and ſticks, they juſtl'd ſide by ſide;

When these did fail, recourse was had to fangs,
And wives full oft' complain'd of direful pangs;
But when the husband prov'd the weaker hand,
The Amazonian female bore command,
Like Russia's Empress, absolute her sway
Within her narrow province; all obey
Her fierce commands, the menial train perform,
For well they know her tonuge and hands can
    storm
The honest husband, settl'd in his chair,
Glad if his fair one brook'd his presence there.—
Long fought they thus, till tir'd at last they yield,
Nor more can Luxury support his shield;
'Twixt their contending armies then was heard
The trumpet sound; a herald next appear'd,
His peaceful sceptre 'twixt their arms he rear'd:
Then mild he spoke, " each army hear my words,
And sheathe for ever your contentious swords;
Thus my imperial lord desires me tell,
The peaceful tenor of his heavenly will;
A treaty 'twixt each other we will sign,
And our chief minister shall each resign
Our royal favour they have much abus'd;
To their vile purposes our words have us'd;
By flatt'ry smooth'd the way into our heart,
Of our displeasure they shall feel the smart;
Henceforth be banish'd from our royal sight,
To dungeons deep, no more to view the light,

In peace and amity we now shall meet,
And with each other live in concord sweet."
 This league concluded, here they end their broils,
And with each other share their mutual spoils;
The shrivel'd miser now assists the beau,
Who does on w—es and dice his wealth bestow,

ON THREE REMARKABLE OCCURRENCES†.

Venus and Death divided have the prey;
Grim Death one lovely maid has born away,
And, hid forever from Sol's chearing rays,
In the cold duſt her charming form decays.
Acroſs the ſea the winged veſſel flies,
And Iſabella bears to bliſs the eyes
Of her expecting lover on the plains
Of India, whom adverſe fate detains;
Th' impatient youth now beats with love's alarms,
And longs to preſs his charmer in his arms;
Chids the ſwift veſſel's tedious delay,
Bids the rough wind and ſea his will obey.
How wondrous are thy works, all powerful Love!
Who rul'ſt in earth beneath, and heaven above,
In female boſoms wak'ſt heroic fire,
To brave each danger doſt their fouls inſpire.

On the fair banks of Yathon's ſwelling tide,
Where Aberdonia's Earl does reſide;
Their blazing torch behold the Hymen rear,
In nuptial tyes a youth and fair appear.

† The *Death* of one, the *Exportation* of another, and the *Marriage* of a third, of the moſt celebrated *Beauties* of Aberdeen.

Thrice happy pair, who Virtue's laws obey,
Nor yield to paſſion's fierce tyrannic ſway;
In one continu'd calm your years ſhall glide,
With you fair Pleaſure ever ſhall abide;
In ſweet connubial love you'll paſs your days,
While on you Venus ſheds her ſofteſt rays.

VERSES,

WRITTEN ON SEEING THE EXECUTION
OF ROBERT WATT.

>   Ah! little think the gay licentious proud,
>   Whom pleasure, power, and affluence furround;
>   They, who their thoughtlefs hours in giddy mirth,
>   And wanton, often cruel, riot wafte;
>   Ah! little think they, while they dance along,
>   How many feel this very moment, Death;
>   And all the fad variety of pain;
>   How many fink in the devouring flood,
>   Or more devouring flame. How many bleed,
>   By fhameful variance betwixt man and man.   Thomson.

Tho' great thy crime, tho' human laws refufe
To grant thee mercy, yet the gentle Mufe
Even over thee may drop a pitying tear,
To pleafe thy fhade and grace thy mournful bier.
Thy guilt fhe hates, yet ftill thy fate deplores,
And hopes thou'lt mercy find on happier fhores.
Sure no State Zealot will accufe her lays,
Which to humanity alone fhe pays;

She grieves for guilt, for virtue's cause she mourns,
No party-rage in her calm bosom burns;
Alike connected with the human race,
She feels their woes, and pities their disgrace.

Unhappy Britain! why should factious rage
Thy sons mislead, or in wild plans engage?
Ah! why should Discord, under Freedom's guise
Lead men each social Virtue to despise;
Lead them, like beasts, by power alone to sway,
While subjects, not by love, but fear, obey!
How different this from Britain's happy laws,
Which want no advocate to plead their cause;
Which virtue guard, nay, even their power ex-
    tend
To crimes, and even criminals defend:—
Till guilty found, the fated head o'ershade,
Nor without evidence will doom him dead.
Which even a Monarch's vices can command,
And from destructive plans withhold his hand.
Can this be bondage? where even Kings obey,
And law alone bears universal sway.   (spise?

And are there found who even these laws de-
Unbounded licence who above them prize?
Let such to Gallia's plains their views direct,
There see their fate who such mild laws reject;
See how her Cities, drench'd in floods of gore,
Mistaken Freedom's furious rage deplore;

See, mild Religion with a sigh retires,
And with her flies each Virtue, or expires;
See licenc'd Murder Freedom's name profane,
And boldly use his dagger, ax, or chain;
While 'neath his feet the regal sceptre bows,
The crown invests his blood-bestained brows.

When such the scene, can any human mind
For crimes like these a fate too odious find?
Such crimes as these, unhappy man! were thine,
Such were thy plans, and such thy dire design!
But Britain's happier Genius wards the blow,
And justly lays the proud oppressor low.
May then thy fate an awful fear impart,
To each disloyal and dishonest heart,
That those who scorn the nobler band of *Love*,
May, by the meaner motive, *Fear* improve.

THE MODERN HERO.

Arma virumque cano.   Virg.
Arms, and the man, I sing.

Late, as sage Homer's leaves I turn'd,
I with poetic ardour burn'd,
And, deeply stung with jealous ire,
To imitate his noble fire,
I thus resolv'd :—Be it decreed,
I'll even Homer's fire exceed;
Adventroufly I'll give to fame,
What in his days had not a name.
Had Homer known the Heroes I
Would thus exalt unto the sky,
He would have spar'd my pains, and won
The bays from me, an humble drone.
But since to the poetic Nine,
Unknown our modern Heroes shine,
I will the character explain,
As best I can, in humble strain.
   Come, Muses Nine, my breast inspire,
And rightly tune my sounding lyre;
Come, gentle spirit, come away,
Who arm'st thy heroe for the fray;

And with heroic ardour bright,
Sustains his nerves amid the fight.
Thus I, supported, will rehearse,
As Homer did, in lofty verse,
The wondrous acts each hero did,
Which credibility excceed.

Now modern day approach'd, and now,
Out struts each well appointed beau.;
But first observe his armour bright,
Which does reflect pure Cynthia's light;
His sword, O wondrous! two ells long!
Which does denote him mighty strong;
Which saucy air at 's belt it hangs,
And on his thigh terrific bangs.
Next, see his hand fast grasps a bludgeon,
With which, when he's in any gudgeon,
Like Hercules he lays about him,
And yet he swears 'tis all for whim.
Oft' does the watchman's batter'd scull,
Declare for bruising his good will;
Nor can frail glass, or lamps withstand him,
But down he thumps them all at random.
Thus, while the fumes of good port wine
His airy spirit do refine,
And make his body debonair,
He does address him to the fair;
By gentle methods first he tries them,
That he may in love's net surprize them.

If that wont do, perforce they yield,
No fraud from his embrace can shield;
Thro' doors and bolts he quickly flies,
And to the fair one's chamber hies;
There in embraces close he holds her,
And in his loving arms infolds her;
Thus in soft raptures pass'd the night,
Up now he starts with dawn of light,
And to his bed-room weari'd hies,
Where balmy slumbers close his eyes.
   At death a scoffer tho' he be,
Yet conscience stings him like a flea;
How often with her lash she twangs,
And in his breast awakes dire pangs.
She asks him, why he shuns the light,
Nor from his bed departs till night?
While other mortals rest, why he
Is then all action, then all glee?
Why Cynthia chuse, when Sol all day
Illumes the world with his bright ray?
Why chuse t' embrace such foolish errors,
Which strip the future of its terrors?
To this he answers with a sigh;
Dame Conscience, I will tell you why:—
If I religion and such stuff
Should mind, then fashion takes the huff,
And at me all the world would jeer,
And say, I did so but thro' fear;

Mov'd by dull fear, I'm not, indeed;
'Tis quite againſt my fixed creed ;
The preſent 's all the heaven I have,
Then to the future I'm no ſlave ;
So Conſcience huſh, down, down, ye jade;
Leſt with your ſtuff you make me mad.

THE BIRTH OF BEAUTY. A FABLE.
VERSIFIED FROM THE TATLER.

When the fantastic changeful maid,
Beauty, on earth her charms display'd;
Jove with a feast did hail her birth,
And bade men's sons join in his mirth:
The God of Plenty with these guests,
On every delicacy feasts ;
He at the board his form display'd,
And gladly drank health to the maid ;
Then having plenteous liquors quaff'd,
And having sung, and having laugh'd ;
Into Jove's garden he retir'd,
Where Somnus with rich wine conspir'd;
To throw soft slumbers o'er his eyes;
There prostrate in a bower he lies.
 Meanwhile, the news of this grand treat;
Reach'd even Poverty's retreat ;
Who, having come, with eager haste,
Hoping to share in the repast,
Thro' Jove's sweet garden took her way ;
Where, spying Plenty as he lay,

T

She's dazled with his blooming charms,
And fondly clafp'd him in her arms;
The God awoke, but being drunk,
He took her for fome wanton punk;
Soon he accomplifh'd her defire,
And fatisfi'd her am'rous fire.
From this embrace, a child there fprung,
Whofe tricks we poets oft have fung;
Yet we have all miftook his kin,
And laid on Venus' back the fin.
Whether the imp be blind or no,
He feldom miffes with his bow;
He fometimes pierces maidens hearts,
But ofteft throws at men his darts.

EXTEMPORE,

ON " AVARUS SEMPER EGIT."

A STUBBORN fellow did refuse,
To own me favour'd of the Muse;
And when a theme he had colegit,
Which was " *avarus semper egit.*"
He bade me, in an half hour's time,
Give him on it a proper rhyme.
I thus began. " O friendly Muse,
Do'nt now thy needful aid refuse,
Let me convince this silly blockhead,
That I'm thy favourite, indeed."
I scarcely these few words had spoke,
I scarcely did the Muse invoke;
When instant fav'ring fancy teems,
And brings for instance C * * * * * * W * * * * *;
Who, in the midst of plenty 's needy,
The more he has, who 's still more greedy;
While I expose his goods for sale,
Fearful he views the wavering scale;
He on the balance keeps his eye,
And when it falls, lets fall a sigh;

On thefe occafions he is *femper*
Unable to command his temper;
But cries out, in a horrid fright,
" WILLIAM, why give you fo much weight?"
I anfwer, " Sir, I need not tell,
That fcanty weighers go to hell;
Wherefore, the fear of my own foul,
The weights and fcales muft ftill controul."
" Fie, filly boy, hold your peace,"
He crys, " and from fuch pratting ceafe;
If we our neighbours do not cheat,
We ne'er fhall feel hell's fcorching heat."

 I hope now, WILLIAM, you'll believe,
That I the Mufes aid receive;
I hope this credit will obtain,
And you'll not trouble me again.

LINES
ADDRESSED
TO MISS N **** T ****, ABERDEEN.

Were 't not that N * * * already warms
My panting breast with love's alarms;
To Nancy's charms I'd yield my soul;
To Nancy's health I'd fill the bowl;
To Nancy's praise I'd form the lay,
And bid the Muse each charm display,
Which in sweet Nancy's features glows,
Whose cheeks excel the damask rose;
Whose eyes the bright ætherial blue,
And every sparkling star, outdo;
Whose snowy bosom gently swells,
Ah! there, ye youths, what rapture dwells;
Whose crimson lips and taper waist,
Shew graces not to be express'd;
Whose flaxen tresses, like my N ****,
Each other maid's, save her's excels.
Can then we doubt, when thus array'd,
A virtuous soul informs the maid?
Can then we doubt, that decent pride
Does o'er each action still preside?

For what, alas! is outward grace?
What all the beauties of the face?
What is the tincture of the skin,
If hideous vice presides within?
Curs'd, then, be he who dares deform
With vicious fraud, the female form!
Curs'd be the vile, the selfish joy,
Which its dear object dares destroy.
But hail! thou holy, heavenly flame,
'Tis thou alone deserv'st the name,
The sacred name of virtuous love,
Which reason aids, which saints approve.

PARNASSUS AT HOME.

Late, as I mufing up ftairs trode,
Unto my lofty night abode,
The firft thing that there ftruck mine eyes,
Half petrifi'd me with furprize;
Me-thought my table turn'd a mount,
From midft of which ran a black fount;
The papers on't were chang'd to trees,
Whofe verdant colours well might pleafe.
What need we, then, fo far to roam,
Parnassus we can find at home.
As for the fam'd Pierian fpring,
Of which the fab'ling poets fing;
Each man may have it by his lug,
'Tis fimply this, a full ink jug.

THE WISH.

Be this my praife, my monumental lay,
When I the fummons of ftern fate obey;
Long liv'd he quiet mid' a world of ftrife,
And ufeful was his every day of life;
Strict to the path of Virtue he adher'd,
Nor Vice, tho' deck'd in robes of ftate, rever'd.

LINES
ADDRESSED TO A YOUNG LADY.
WRITTEN AT THE DESIRE OF A FRIEND.

Cælia, dear partner of my youthful heart,
   This tribute to thy blooming charms I pay,
Whose gentle influence, devoid of art,
   The Muse awakes, and prompts the willing lay.

From thee remote, the tedious hours I count,
   And wish in vain thy lovely eyes to meet;
Perhaps some lofty eminence I mount,
   In hopes the western coast mine eyes will greet.

When evening comes, array'd in sober gray,
   To thee, with each declining sun, I send
My ardent wishes in some pensive lay,
   That Heaven thy every step would still befriend.

Even now, reclin'd on ARTHUR's lofty SEAT,
  Where seas and skies in mingled prospect ly;
I recollect my former dear retreat,
  And view my CÆLIA there with fancy's eye.

Around her waist, methinks, my arms I twine,
  While her fair bosom heaves to meet my view;
I cry, my CÆLIA, thou shalt still be mine.
  And thus around thee still my arms I'll glue.

In HYMEN's bands united, we shall prove
  The purest pleasure of the human mind;
The blissful joys of sweet connubial love
  Our hearts, our interests, shall together bind.

Ah! dear delusions of all potent Love,
  Why thus my troubled bosom still disturb?
Who knows if CÆLIA may my suit approve,
  Or, pleas'd, survey the passion I can't curb.

Thus as I mus'd, disclos'd in open view,
  The Goddess Hope before mine eyes appear'd,
Bade me my wishes and my vows renew,
  And all the prospect in a moment clear'd.

On me she smil'd, and thus the Goddess said,
  Let CÆLIA know your constancy and love;
Impart your passion to the charming Maid,
  Perhaps yourself and suit she may approve.

Encourag'd thus, I snatch'd my willing quill,
  The Muse invok'd to aid Love's gentle cause;
And thus the Goddess' orders I fulfill,
  And crave no laurel but my Fair's applause.

ODE TO HOPE.

O GENTLE POWER, whose smiles still smooth
The rugged paths of life to youth;
Who human sorrows canst assuage,
And calm tumultuous passion's rage.
Hope, smiling Hope, come to my breast,
   And soothe the anguish there!
If thou art not, I am depress'd,
   By gloomy, dire Despair.
The tyrant foul, with scouling brow,
   O'er me usurps domain;
He frowns terrific on me now,
   And wrings my soul with pain.
Where, Heavenly Muses, where your boasted
       power?
O aid your vot'ry, in this dark, this dismal hour.

Ah! what avails the tuneful lyre,
Or what tho' Phœbus' self inspire;
Yet that not shields from woe,
Nor can even Phœbus ward the blow.

Nay, rather, whom the Mufes aid,
  Still feel affliction's power;
Nor one who e'er to Phœbus pray'd,
  But it's fharp pangs has bore;
And groan'd beneath the cruel weight,
  Of anguifh and defpair;
Or for a fhip with riches freight,
  Or for a haughty fair;
The one the raging foaming ocean tore;
The other, cruel fate from their embraces bore.

Thus equally by grief deprefs'd,
We feek at laft for quiet reft,
Amid fome beauteous rural bower,
And there we court the foothing power,
Of folitude and gentle eafe,
  Which calm the tempeft of our mind,
And teach the fcenes of life to pleafe,
  As far's they ought, tho' here we find,
Like ocean's wave, unftable blifs,
  And figh for bowers of endlefs joy,
Where no deception harbour'd is,
  And where no cares the breaft annoy;
Where Virtue wipes all forrows from our eyes,
And full perfection reigns above the fkies.

POEMS

IN THE

SCOTTISH DIALECT.

EPISTLES.

EPISTLE I.

TO MR JOHN MOIR, PRINTER, EDINBURGH.

Here, Sir, I fen' thae scrawls o' mine,
In hopes ye'll print them unco fine;
An' by my saul, gin weil ye do't,
Ye never s'all hae cause to rue't;
For I sall pay you leel an' sicker,
An' as we can'no hae a bicker,
Foul fa' me bat I'se be a lown,
Gin I no spen' a hale half-crown,
To drink your health wi' a' my heart,
An' gude speed to you i' your art;
O mony a buiky may you get,
An' mony a typie may you set;
Till tir'd at last o' wark an' siller,
Whan nae ae pouchie can be filler,
Ye may gi'e o'er to wirk an' drudge,
An' spen' your groat without a grudge.

Gin riches be your lot, I'm sure
Ye'll no be ill to folk that's poor;
For weel I wyte, ye ha'e the heart,
To sic as need it to impart;
As I mysel am very sure,
Cud witness fan I was right poor.
But here your bounty was beguil'd,
An' a' your kin' attention foil'd,
In helpin' o' a thriftless chiel,
Whom ilk ane ca's a ne'er-do-weil.
An', by my saul, I fear it's true,
Gin printin' do no' help me now;
But gin the buiky weil sud sell,
Fat I may come to nane can tell;
For wi it's profits, gin I'm spar'd,
I yet may chance to be a laird.
Sae, my guid frien', be busy man,
An' whan the siller comes to han',
Ye sall get something worth your pains,
For 'tis but right ye share my gains.

EPISTLE II.
TO MR ALEXANDER SCOTT,
SCHOOL-MASTER, BALLHILL.

Thanks, Sandy Scott, for the braw Bitch
Ye've gi'en me, an' whan I grow rich,
O'er a guid cog o' gin an' water,
Wi' you I'fe hae a canty clatter;
We'll foon forget bauld Fortune's nips,
Which aft ha'e gripit Bardie's hips.
We'll jaw about the Mufe, an' chat
O' high Parnassus, an' a' that:
An' fyne we'll gi'e our pow a claw,
An maybe try a verfe or twa;
For gin an' ale can fyles infpire
Mair Bards than Phœbus fel' can fire;
Bat fin' the Mufe an' me forgather'd,
She never gat me fairly tether'd;
For gin it came no i' my noddle,
For her I wad no care a boddle.
An' aye fan't ftricks me i' the pow,
I light, or elfe drown out her low;

For I wad had him but a fool,
Wha wis to her jift like a tool,
That whan she liket she mith ufe,
Or whan she liket mith refufe:
Bat, fegs, o' her I hae fma' pleafure,
Except whan I ha'e fouth o' leifure.
At fick an orow idle time,
I whiles may fcrawl a fcreed o' rhyme;
Bat whan my wark comes i' the gate,
I fling a' frae me in a pet,
Min' naething bat to rooze my bales,
An' ply wi' heart an han' my fcales,
Till gather'd wivies fwear their purfe
Is light, an' maybe lat a curfe,
That they ha'e coft fae mickle gear;
An' fay, guid fegs, I'm in a fear,
That the gudeman at hame 'll fcauld,
An' fay, fegs, 'oman, ye're o'er bauld,
To fpen' in merchan's shops the gear
That I ha'e wrought for late an' air.
Says I, hoot 'oman, blefs you, ftop,
I ha'e na cheatit you, I hope;
I gi'en you fouth o' tea an' fuckar,
An' lawn an' gauze to men' your tucker;
Sae 'oman fa' no in ill teens,
For here's a pickle braw ftout prins,
To had your plaid or bufk your gown,
Whan ye gang o'er to the kirk town.

sick cracks as thae can cure a snarle,
An' help a chiel thro' this wile warle,
Whare flatt'ry, an' a heap o' lies,
By far the griter num'er pleafe;
Whare truth is hish'd awa' frae fouk;
Whare friendship's guided like a joke;
Whare love for gowd is coft an' fauld,
An' whare a' guidnefs is grown cauld.
Here o' this fcrawl I mak' an en'
An fign, wi' a' my heart,—your frien'.

P. S. Your Bitchie's praife I canna fpeak,
She's to my trock an unco' eek;
For aye fan I tak' ony anger,
Or am maift fleepin', for meer langour,
She bobs an' loups about me fae,
She flegs baith fleep an' fpleen away;
An' fyne fhe fleeps juft i' my bofie,
For Phœbe kens whare fhe'll be cofie,
An' aye whan ony body chaps
At the fhop door, up Phœbe fnaps,
An' barks aye till fhe waken me,
To fell my fukar an' my tea.

EPISTLE III.

TO THE REVIEWERS.

Right Noble Gentlemen, I true,
Ye maybe may my wark review,
Bat be na over capernoitit,
For mony o' them were indited
Wi' nae intent that ye fud fee them;
Frae fauts an' flaws I winna frie them;
But yet o' this I'm vera fure,
Virtue and truth need never fear,
That I fud ever be their foe,
Or ever gi'e them caufe of woe.
Sae ye may fpare me, gin ye like,
For ye ne'er faw a maftiff tyke
Wad ftan' an' wory at a whelp.
Tho' he in's teeth fud girn an' yelp.
Bat, vow, I wyte I had forgot
I a' this time fpake like a Scot,
Whafe language ye can hardly fpell,
Tho' fome o' you be Scots yourfel';
An' weil I wyte, I'm unco kedgie,
For I'd be laith to difoblige ye.

Sae, gin ye dinna like my fangs,
Be nae o'er heavy wi' your bangs,
An' I fall do my beft to bide ye,
For, well I wyte, I dare no chide ye.
Tho' ye fud even brack my banes,
Or fell me freely wi' your ftanes.

EPISTLE IV.

TO MR ALEXANDER SCOTT,
SCHOOL-MASTER, BALLHILL.

Dear Scottie, troth it's unco lang,
Sine I heard frae ye, by my fang;
Ye furely think I'm nae your frien',
Elfe lang e'er now I wad hae feen
A letter faulded up wi' care,
An' fpell'd an' written unko fair:
Bat I cud lay you ony wager,
I, even the lowmin o' a gauger,
That I amaift the caufe cud guefs,
Why Sandy Scott fae filent is.
O Sandy, troth ye're bat a fool,
To feik awa' wi' a poor fchool,
Whafe winnins wad no buy, tho' better,
As meikle paper's write a letter,
Bat now an' than to a guid frien',
Whom maybe it's lang fine ye ha'e feen;
An' wha right glad wad be to hear
Ye were increas'd in grace and gear.

Now Modesty's nae worth a leek,
Gin ye wad ha'e, troth ye maun seek;
Tak' my advice, an' nae refuse,
To pit this scry into the news.

 A Dominy does want a place,
Wha can baith sing an' say a grace,
Wha even a sermon can indite,
An' sae it's clear the man can write;
Wha counting, writing, latin teaches,
An' gin it's needfu', prays an' preaches:
A' thae guid gifts he has, an mair,
Than in a scry he cud declare.
Gin ony body wants this man,
Pit twenty guineas in his han',
An' gi'e him deed and gift right clearly,
Ye'll pay him this sma' stipend yearly;
Wi' bed an' board, an' a clean sark,
He'll un'ertak to do your wark;
An' whan ye want him, will be ready
To leave for you his aunt or daddy.
This, my dear frien' is my advice,
An' gin ye think o'er sma' the price,
To which your wages I ha'e stentit,
Ye may ca't double whan ye print it.

MISCELLANIES

IN THE

SCOTTISH DIALECT.

MISCELLANIES.

EPILOGUE,

SPOKEN AT THE REPRESENTATION OF

THE TRAGEDY OF DOUGLAS,

AT SLAINS.

WE'LL Sirs, we're dane, fat ha'e ye a' to fay,
I think we've acted gayly this braw Play;
Gin ye're content, I'fe mak but little din,
Tho' I'd fain pit you in a merry pin
Afore I leave you freely. — It's the vogue
To fic braw fhows to gi'e an Epilogue.
Fat think ye, Sirs, o' fic a tragic core,
Wha never acted on a ftage afore.
An' as I'm dane wi' a' my waefu' cracks,
Like a leel Merchan' I'll gae lift my packs.
But e'er I do't, I fain wad ha'e your ear,
To hear a fyle the roozing o' my ware.
Wha wad ha'e thought, that Randolph held the
 plough,
Or wis the fin o' honeft William Touch.

An' now, we'll jift ftap o'er ayont the bogg,
To tell ye Douglas is plain Geordy Hogg.
Fu' we'll ye ken the ale-wife o' the town,
Wha 's mither to Glenalvon, that great lown.
Auld Norval's dady is a fturdy fmith,
Wha yarks at iron goads wi' a' his pith.
My faithfu' Anna is the parfon's fin.
An' for myfel', I fanna vouft my kin,
There's no ane here, but kens the Merchin' weil;
To tell the truth, he's bat a ram'lin' chiel;
An' fegs I'm fear't he mith as well hae dane,
Gin in Auld Chrifty's houfie he had been
Sellin' his gear to fome braw canty wife,
Winnin' a penny to had in his life.
But gin ye'll a' wi' him gang o'er the gate,
A fouth o' pigs an groceries ye fall get;
An' as ye've come to fee his tragic pranks,
For this kin' vifit tak his hearty thanks.

ELEGY,

TO THE MEMORY OF
A FAVOUITE BITCH.

Fat muckle forrow gart you dee,
I'm very sure it was no me;
For, well I wyte, that cud no be,
    Ye wis my dear.
Becaufe your like I cud no fee,
    Nor far nor near.

O Phœbe, my dear bonny bitch,
Foul fa' me but I wis no rich,
Afore ye died, bat or Death's fwitch,
    Had crack'd your crown,
Tho't wad ha'e gi'en my purfe a twitch,
    I'd tint a crown.

Vow bat ye was a bonny dogie,
An' fyne ye wis fae unko vogie,
An' cokit fae your little lugie,
    An' aye wis glad;
To trudge wi' me thro' burn or bogie,
    Thro' guid or bad.

Foul fa' me bat whan 'twas my lot,
To get ye frae my frien' San' Scott,
My fegs I did no care a groat,
     For ony curr,
That ever lickit iron pot,
     Or ga'e a wirr.

O Phœbe, fat cud temp ye fae,
To work yourfel' fo muckle wae,
As gars ye ly baith cauld an' blae,
     Into the groun',
Ye wis o'er young by mony a day,
     To die fo fhoon.

O whare wis Juno i' that hour,
My Phœbe needed fair her power,
To help her thro' the dreadfu' ftour
     O' kleckin' tykes,
An fhe can do't, I'm vera fure,
     Aye whan fhe likes.

For fhe's a howdie o' renown,
Wha wis employ'd by ilka lown,
That dwalt in ony Grecian town,
     Or far or near,
Tho', by my fegs, I jift maun own
     Her wage wis dear.

Tho' my dear Phœbe's gane frae me,
This Elegy to her s'all gi'e
Renown an' fame, o'er lan' an' fea,
     Gin it ware printit,
An' Phœbe's name s'all never die,
     This s'all prevent it.

AN ADDRESS,

INTENDED TO HAVE BEEN PRINTED

ON THE OPENING OF

THE AUTHOR's CIRCULATING LIBRARY,

AT PETERHEAD.

Here's Willie Farquhar's hinmoſt ſhift,
At a' thing elſe he had no thrift:
Come in then, lads, an gi'e 'm a lift,
    His buiks are bonny,
An' ye may plainly ſee his drift,
    Is to mak' money.

Gin ilka chiel in Peterhead,
Wad come to 's ſhop for buiks to read,
He ſud get warks wad fill his head
    Wi' thrifty notions;
Or, gin he thought it wis as guid,
    Wi' ſleepy potions.

For Authors are like ither men,
They dinna a' tak' up the pen,
Wi' an intent their win' to ſpen',
    To mak' ye vogie,
Bat ſometimes ſleepin' recommen',
    As weil's a cogie.

Bat there are unco few o' mine,
That are o' this wile dozen'd kin :
Na, they are buiks that fill the min',
     Nae wi' fool buft,
Bat wi' Benevolence divine,
     An' fic guid ftuff.

HORACE, BOOK I. ODE XXVI. IMITATED

A FRIEN' to the Mufes, I will dread nae fkaith,
A' fears to the win's I gi'e o'er and bequeath,
Being even right carelefs fat King's dreaded
   breath
      Comman's the pole,
I ne'er fafh my pow, gin GEORDY fears Death,
      For that he maun thole.

O Mufe, whofe delight is to hear burnies hurl,
A garlan' mak' ready for N**** bonny curl,
Whafe praife, wi' thy aid, s'all ring thro' the
   world,
      An' mak' immortal,
The laffie whafe een even faften the churl,
      An' pleafe ilka mortal.

MISCELLANIES.

SONG.

Says Johnny, were my Anny mine,
　　I'd ilk misfortune scorn;
Riches wi' ease I cud resign,
　　An' blythesome rise ilk morn.

Wi' virr my loomy I wad turn,
　　To win my Annie's bread;
An' for my wark seek nae return,
　　Gin she an' I agreed.

Syne gallop fast, an' bring the day
　　Whan she'll gi'e me her han';
Syne, gin ye like, a month it may
　　Be dark o'er a' our lan'.

At even, whan I gi'e o'er the wark,
　　To her I rin wi' haste,
To get a walk into the park,
　　An' clasp her roun' the waist.

Her presence mak's me brisk an' gay,
　　An' syne, wi' mony a vow,
I swear, I'll faithfu' be for aye,
　　An' pree her bonny mow.

Were't no her, my prentice years
    Had been o'er lang indeed;
Bat now I drop right mony tears,
    An' wis' no to be freed.

At F———— I now wad stay,
    Bat Fortune winna lat me;
An' I maun turn anither way,
    An' live wi' her that gat me.

Bat, weil I wyte, my mither dear,
    Gin ye'd no angry be,
Tho' ye are kin', I'm very sure,
    Ye're nae sae kin' as she.

Bat shortly, whan I've made some wheels,
    I'll gang for A**** P*****;
She'll gi'e an edge to a' my tools,
    She's be my wife expressly.

Sae, mither, ye may had your tongue,
    An' never fash your beard,
Nor plague us that we are o'er young,
    Wi' that we's nae be scar'd.

www.ingramcontent.com/pod-product-compliance
Lightning Source LLC
Chambersburg PA
CBHW020914230426
43666CB00008B/1453